WHS

national TESTS practice papers

FOR THE YEAR 2002

Maths, English and Science

Book 1

practice Papers

AGE

13-14

Key Stage 3

Acknowledgements
The authors and publisher would like to thank the following for permission to reproduce material in this book.

Gunpowder Plot, Robson Books Ltd 1994
London Labour and the London Poor, Henry Mayhew, ed. Victor E. Newburg, Penguin Books 1985

Every effort has been made to trace and acknowledge ownership of copyright material but if any have been inadvertently overlooked, the publisher will be pleased to make the necessary alterations at the first opportunity.

First published 2001
exclusively for WHSmith by

Hodder & Stoughton Educational,
a division of Hodder Headline Ltd
338 Euston Road
London NW1 3BH

A CIP record for this book is available from the British Library.

Authors: Steve Mills and Hilary Koll (Maths), Christine Moorcroft and Ray Barker (English), Terry Hudson (Science)

ISBN 0340 84590 2

Printed and bound by Graphycems, Spain

NOTE: The tests, questions and advice in this book are not reproductions of the official test materials sent to schools. The official testing process is supported by guidance and training for teachers in setting and marking tests and interpreting the results. The results achieved in the tests in this book may not be the same as are achieved in the official tests.

Contents

Introduction

The National Tests – A summary

What are the National Tests?

Children who attend state schools in England and Wales sit National Tests (commonly known as SATs) at the ages of 7, 11 and 14, usually at the beginning of May. They may also sit optional tests in the intervening years – many schools have chosen to adopt these tests. The test results are accompanied by an assessment by the child's teacher (at Key Stage 3 this also covers non-tested subjects such as History or Geography).

The results are used by the school to assess each child's level of knowledge and progress in English and Maths at Key Stage 1 and English, Maths and Science at Key Stages 2 and 3. They also provide useful guidance for the child's next teacher when he or she is planning the year's work.

The educational calendar for children aged 5-14 is structured as follows:

Key Stage	Year	Age by end of year	National Test
1 (KS1)	1	6	
	2	7	KEY STAGE 1
2 (KS2)	3	8	Optional Year 3
	4	9	Optional Year 4
	5	10	Optional Year 5
	6	11	KEY STAGE 2
3 (KS3)	7	12	
	8	13	
	9	14	KEY STAGE 3

Levels

National targets have been set for children's results in the National Tests. The levels are set as follows:

LEVEL	AGE 7	AGE 11	AGE 14
8			
7			
6			
5			
4			
3			
2 2a 2b 2c			
1			

BELOW EXPECTED LEVEL

EXPECTED LEVEL

ABOVE EXPECTED LEVEL

EXCEPTIONAL

Results

Your child's school will send you a report indicating his or her levels in the tests and the teacher assessment.

The school's overall test results will be included in local and national league tables, which are published in most newspapers.

What can parents do to help?

While it is never a good idea to encourage cramming, you can help your child to succeed by:

- Making sure he or she has enough food, sleep and leisure time during the test period.
- Practising important skills such as writing and reading stories, spelling and mental arithmetic.
- Telling him or her what to expect in the test, such as important symbols and key words.
- Helping him or her to be comfortable in test conditions including working within a time limit, reading questions carefully and understanding different ways of answering.

Timetable

The Key Stage 1 National Tests are carried out in May. They often form part of a child's normal school day, as they are generally practical and teacher-assessed. Many children at Key Stage 1 do not even realise they are taking a test.

Key Stage 2 tests take place in one week in May. All children sit the same test at the same time. In 2002, the tests will take place in the week of **13–17 May**. Your child's school will be able to provide you with a detailed timetable.

Key Stage 3 students will sit their tests on **7–13 May**, with the following timetable (check with your child's school as dates may change):

Tuesday 7 May	Wednesday 8 May	Thursday 9 May	Friday 10 May	Monday 13 May
MORNING				
English Paper 1 (1½ hours plus 15 minutes reading time)	Mathematics Paper 1 (1 hour)	English Extension Paper (1½ hours)	Science Paper 1 (1 hour)	Science Extension Paper (1 hour)
	Mental Arithmetic Tests A and C (20 minutes)	Mental Arithmetic Test B (20 minutes)		
AFTERNOON				
English Paper 2 (1¼ hours)	Mathematics Paper 2 (1 hour)	Mathematics Extension Paper (1 hour)	Science Paper 2 (1 hour)	

Maths at Key Stage 3

Guidance for parents

The Key Stage 3 Maths test consists of two written papers, one to be taken without a calculator and the other with a calculator, and a mental arithmetic test. The tests will cover aspects of Number and Algebra, Shape, Space and Measures and Handling Data.

Levels and tiers of entry

For mathematics, your child will be entered for one of four tiers. Your child's teacher will make a judgement about which of the tiers to enter your child for, deciding on the tier that best matches their ability.

This book includes two written papers that cover the most popular tiers of entry. Paper 1 covers levels 4–6 and Paper 2 covers levels 5–7. The mental arithmetic test includes questions at levels 4–7. To gain an idea of the level at which your child is working, use the table on page 44, which shows you how to convert your child's marks into a National Curriculum level.

Setting the Maths Tests

Equipment needed

Paper 1: pen, pencil, ruler, rubber,

Paper 2: pen, pencil, ruler, rubber, protractor or angle measurer, pair of compasses, scientific or graphic calculator, tracing paper and a mirror (optional).

Mental Maths Test: pencil and rubber.

A clock or watch with a second hand is useful for ensuring times for each question on the mental test are appropriate.

The written papers

A formula sheet is included for each test. Encourage your child to refer to it where necessary. Each written paper lasts for **1 hour**, starting with easier questions and gradually becoming more difficult.

The mental maths test

The mental test should take approximately **20 minutes** to give. Cut out pages 33–34 so you can read them aloud to your child. Your child should use the sheets on pages 35, 36 and 37 for his or her answers.

Marking the tests

Next to each question in the written tests is a number indicating how many marks the question or part of the question is worth.

Enter your child's mark into the circle above, using the answer pages to help you decide how many points to award.

The answer pages (38–44) also offer advice, provide information about common errors made by pupils and include tips to help your child understand the mathematical ideas.

Find your child's total score from the written papers and refer to page 44 for information about the level at which your child might be working.

Maths Test

Paper 1

Formulae

You cannot use a calculator for any questions in paper 1.

You might need to use these formulae.

AREA

Circle

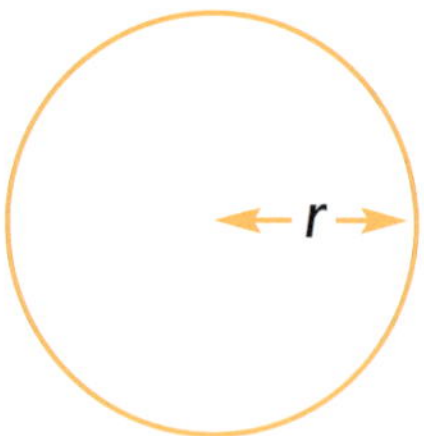

πr^2

Take π as 3.14.

Triangle

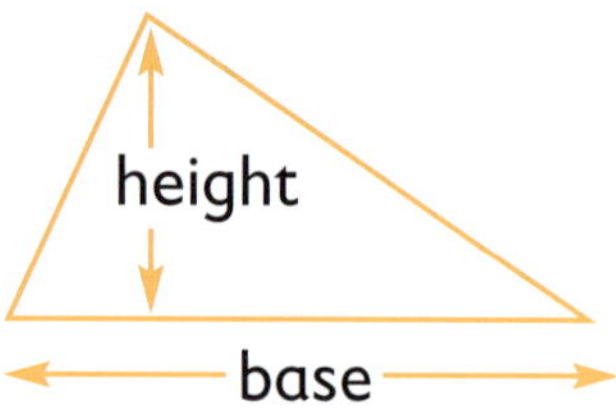

$\dfrac{\text{base} \times \text{height}}{2}$

Parallelogram

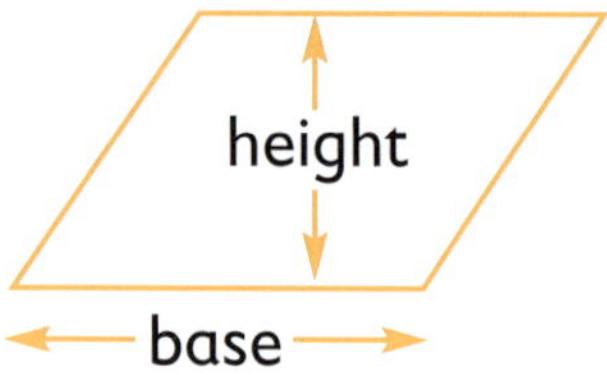

base $\times$ height

Trapezium

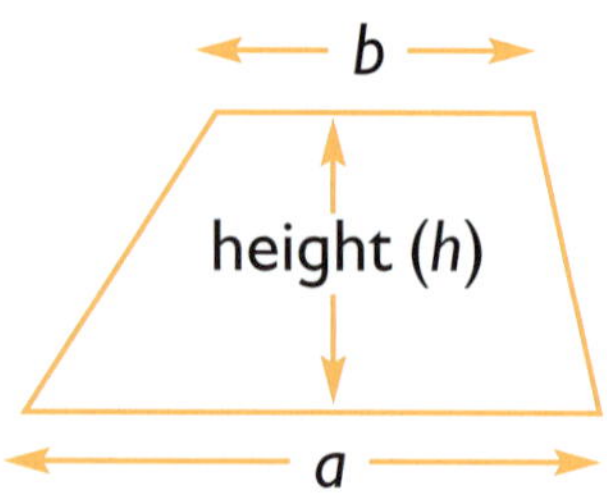

$\dfrac{(a + b)}{2} \times h$

LENGTH

Circle

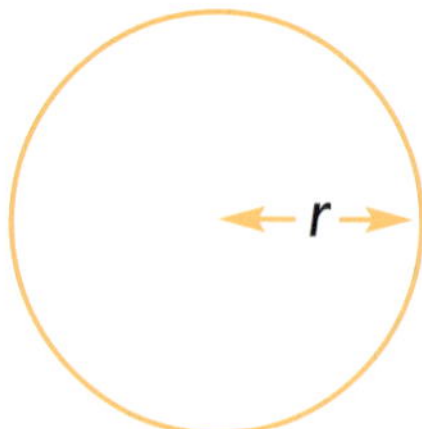

circumference = $2\pi r$

VOLUME

Prism

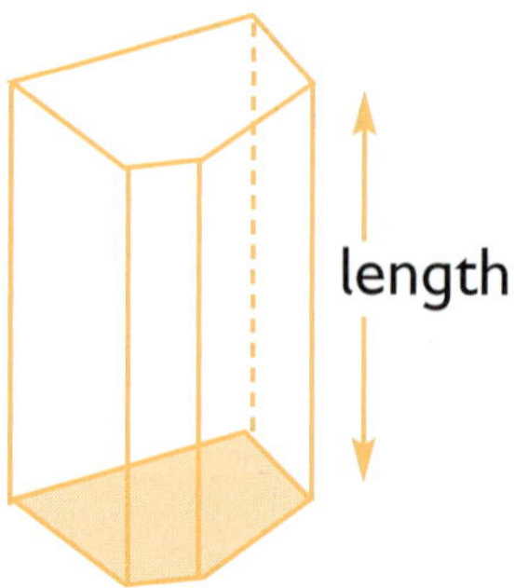

area of cross-section $\times$ length

You will need: pen, pencil, rubber and ruler.

Example

What fraction of this bar of chocolate has been eaten?

$\frac{3}{8}$

a What fraction of this bar of chocolate has been eaten?

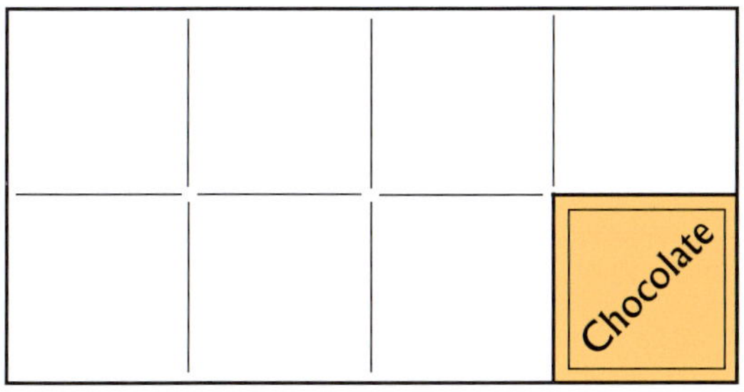

b What fraction of this bar of chocolate has been eaten?
Give your answer in its simplest form.

Fractions and percentages

1 $\frac{1}{2}$ of this bar of chocolate has been eaten.

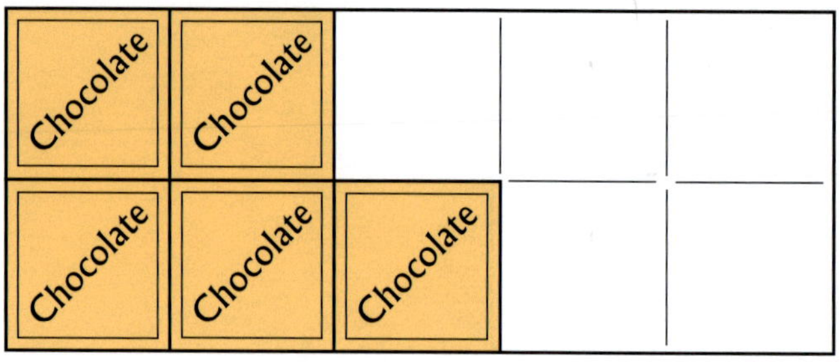

a What fraction of this bar of chocolate has been eaten?

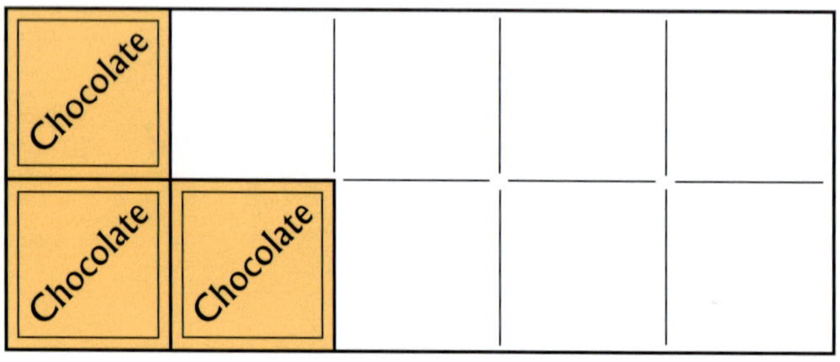

3/10 x 7/10 ✓

1

b What fraction of this bar of chocolate has been eaten?
Give your answer in its simplest form.

3/5 x 2/5 ✓

1

What percentage of the bar has not been eaten?

40% x 60%

1

TOTAL

3

c Shade $\frac{1}{6}$ of this chocolate bar.

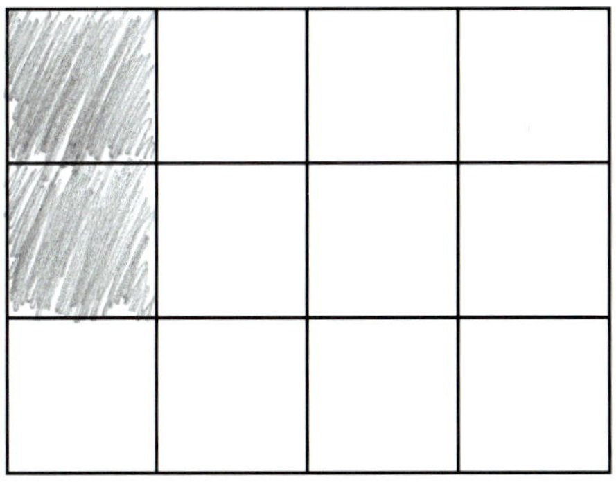

1

d Shade **70%** of the chocolate bar below.

1

TOTAL

2

2

Co-ordinates

2 Shape A has five vertices (corners).

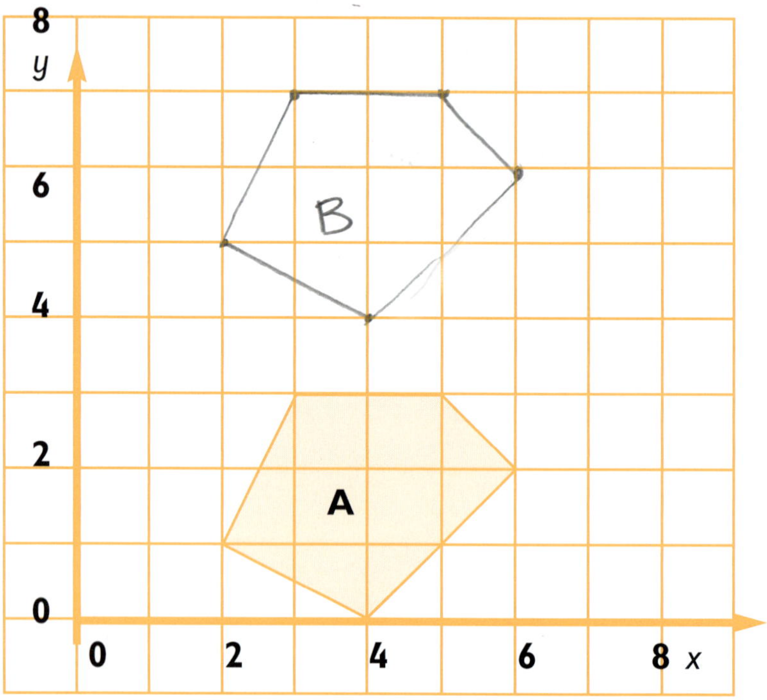

a Write the co-ordinates of the vertices of Shape A in any order.

(4, 0) (2, 1) (3, 3) (5, 3) (6, 2)

✓ 1

Dan has thought of a rule to change the co-ordinates of Shape A.

b Rewrite the co-ordinates, following Dan's rule.

(4, 4) (2, 5) (3, 7) (5, 7) (6, 6)

✓ 1

TOTAL 2 / 2

Now mark the new co-ordinates you have written onto the grid and join them up to make a new shape. Label this shape 'B'.

c Explain how Shape A has been changed to Shape B in your own words.

All of the co-ordinates of the y axis have been moved up 4.

✓ 1

d Dan has thought of a different rule to change the co-ordinates of a shape.

Explain how the shape would be changed if Dan's new rule was followed.

The shape will move left two spaces.

✓ 1

TOTAL 2 / 2

Missing Numbers

3 Write one number in each box to make each equation correct.

a 280 ÷ [8] = 35 ✓ 1

b 1160 ÷ [10] = 116 ✓ 1

c [1133] − 40 = 73 ✓ 1

d [40] × 9 = 360 ✓ 1

e [72] ÷ 8 = 9 ✓ 1

TOTAL 5 / 5

Multiplying

4 The school caretaker needs to find the area of a classroom floor to buy carpet for it. The floor measures **39 feet** by **18 feet**.
This is how he multiplies **18** by **39**.

39 feet

18 feet

	30	9	
10	300	90	390
8	240	72	+ 312
			702

Use the caretaker's method to find the area of a rectangle **15 feet** by **27 feet**.

27 feet

15 feet

	20	7	
10	200	70	270
5	100	35	+ 135
			405

Area of rectangle = 405 square feet

3

TOTAL

3

3

Milk

5 A supermarket shelf holds three types of milk:
full-cream, half-fat and **skimmed**.

There are **8 full-cream**, **12 half-fat and 4 skimmed** milk bottles on the shelf.
Jack picks a bottle from the shelf without looking.

a What is the **probability** that he picks a bottle of **skimmed** milk?
Write your answer as a **fraction** in its simplest form.

4/24 1/6 ✓

1

b Draw a cross on this line to show the probability that Jack picks a bottle of **full-cream** milk.

1

c Draw a cross on this line to show the probability that Jack does **not** pick a bottle of **full-cream** milk.

1

TOTAL 3 / 3

The **first** bottle of milk picked was a bottle of **half-fat** milk.
He puts it in his basket.

Jack now picks a **second** bottle **from the same shelf** without looking.

d Tick which of these three statements is true.

"The next bottle Jack picks is likely to be full-cream."

"The probability of Jack picking a bottle of half-fat milk is the same as before."

"Jack is more likely to pick a bottle of half-fat milk than any other bottle of milk." ✓

Explain your answer.

There are more half-fat bottles than any other kind.

✓ 1

TOTAL 1 / 1

Rainfall

6 This graph shows the rainfall during the first week in March.

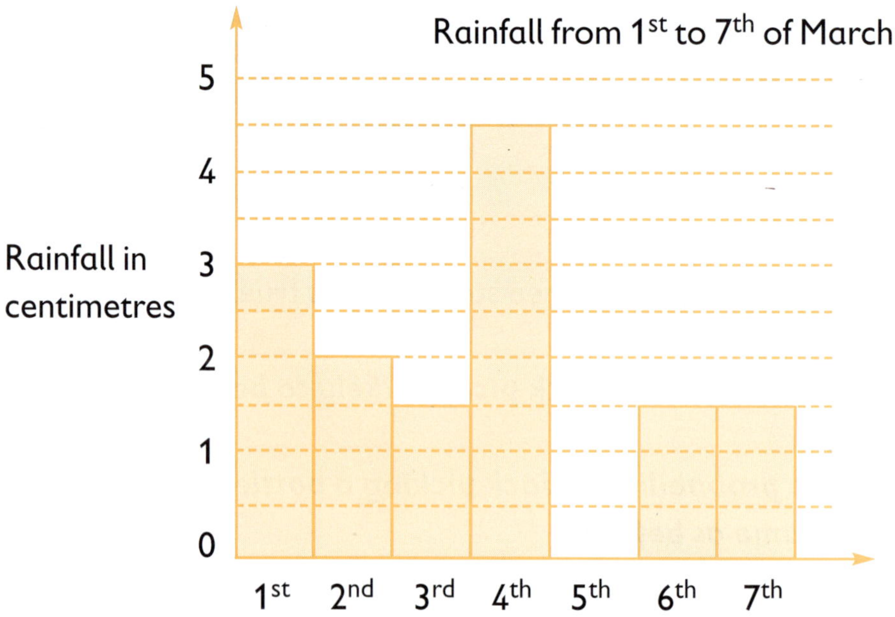

Look at the graph.

a Some of the statements below are true and some are false.

Tick the statements that are **true**.

For three days during this week, the daily rainfall was less than 2 cm.	
For all days during this week, the daily rainfall was 1 cm or more.	
The mean daily rainfall during this week was 2 cm.	✓
The total rainfall during this period was 15 cm.	

✓ 2

TOTAL

2

2

b Calculate the **range** of the daily rainfall from March 1st to March 7th.

$4\frac{1}{2} - 0 = 4\frac{1}{2}$

4.5cm

1

c The rainfall for the following week (from March 8th to March 14th) was also recorded on a graph.
The **mean** daily rainfall for this period was **4 cm**.
Use this information to record the daily rainfall for March 8th.

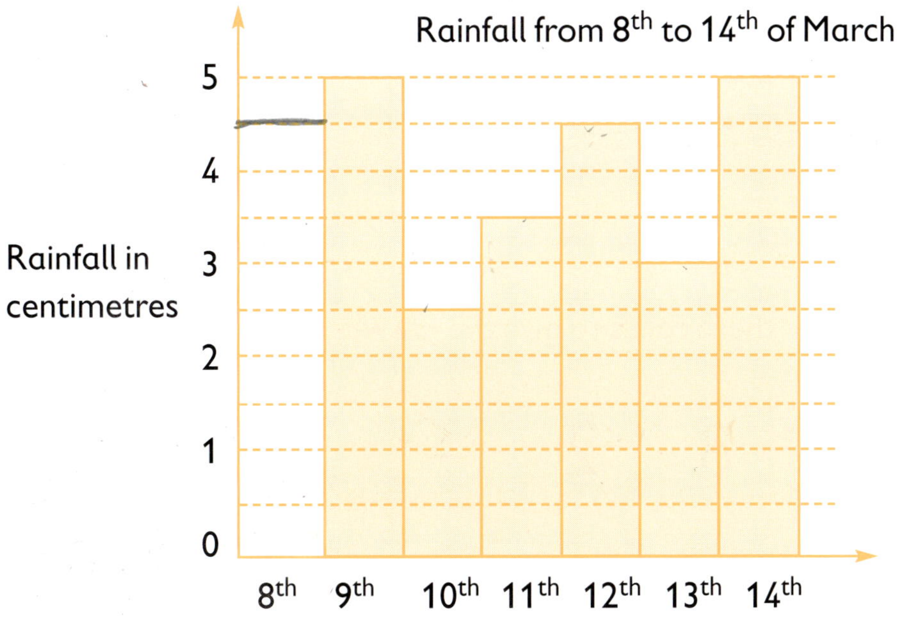

1

d Calculate the mean daily rainfall for the two week period from March 1st to March 14th.

3cm

1

TOTAL

3

3

Negatives

7 Linford has cards with some numbers and signs on. He arranges them to make equations.

Fill in one number in **each** equation below.

a

–5	+	3	=	–2

1

b

7	–	9	+	8	=	6

1

c

6	+	–5	–	2	=	–1

1

d Reorder these cards to give the answer **3**.

–3	8	2	–	+

8	+	-3	–	2	=	3

1

TOTAL 4

4

8a Lee has been given some equations to solve.

$2a + 7 = 19$	$5b - 16 = 24$	$2c^2 + 5 = 37$

Solve the equations to find the values of a, b and c.

$a =$ 6 ✓ $b =$ 8 ✓ $c =$ 8 ✗

2
3

b Lee solves his equations on a rectangular piece of paper.
The **width** of Lee's piece of paper is **8 cm less** than the **length**.

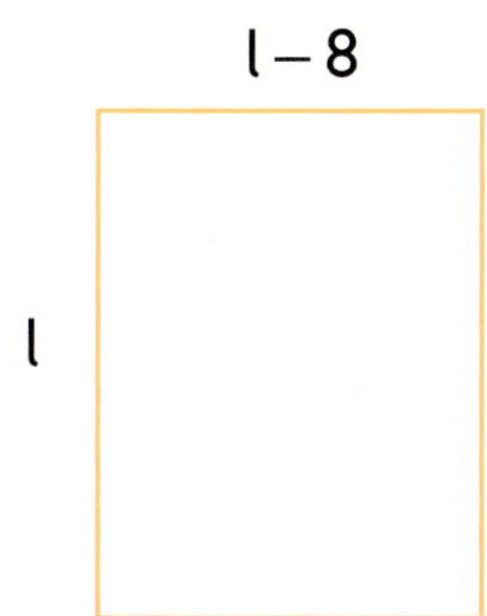

The **perimeter** of his piece of paper is 92 cm.
Calculate the width of the piece of paper.

92 − 16 = 76 ÷ 4 = 19

Width = 19

✓
2

TOTAL
4
5

Fractions

9 A farmer is planting seeds in **32 fields**.

This table shows information about how many fields the farmer is planting each day.

Day	**Number of fields planted**	**Total number of fields planted so far**	**Fraction of total number of fields planted so far**
Monday	1	1	$\frac{1}{32}$
Tuesday	1	2	$\frac{1}{16}$
Wednesday	2	4	$\frac{1}{8}$
Thursday	5		
Friday	10		
Saturday	5		
Sunday		32	1

Complete the table so that it shows, for each day:

- the **number of fields planted**
- the **total number of fields planted**
- the **fraction of the total number of fields planted**

Give all fractions in their simplest form.

5

TOTAL

5

Sequences

10 Here is part of a number grid made from squares. The pattern continues each time by adding a new layer of squares along the bottom edge. Each of the squares in a layer is numbered.

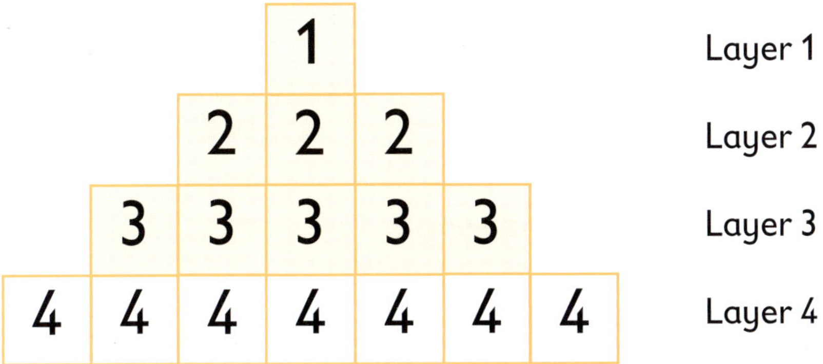

a Calculate how many squares will be in layer 7.

13

1

b Complete the table.

Layer	1	2	3	4	10
Number of squares in layer	1	3	5	7	19

1

c Write an expression to show the number of squares in layer ***n***.

1

d How many squares in all the layers **altogether** would there be in a model with ***n*** layers?

2

TOTAL

2

5

Maths Test

Paper 2

Formulae

You can use a calculator for any questions in paper 2.

You might need to use these formulae.

AREA

Circle

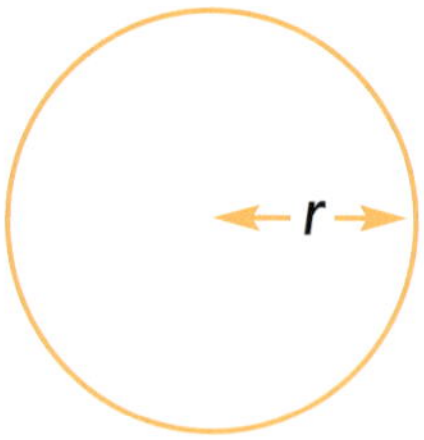

πr^2

Take π as 3.14 or use the π button on your calculator.

Triangle

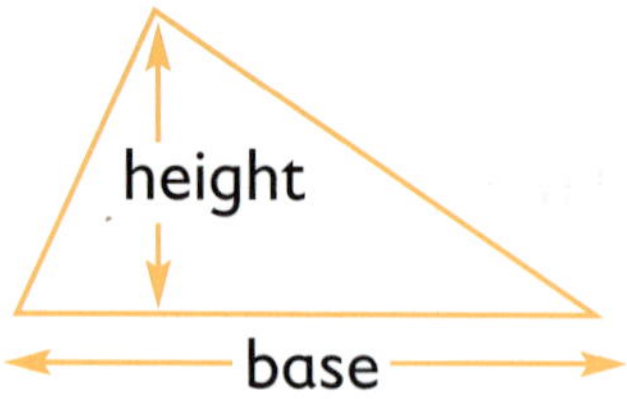

$\frac{\text{base} \times \text{height}}{2}$

Parallelogram

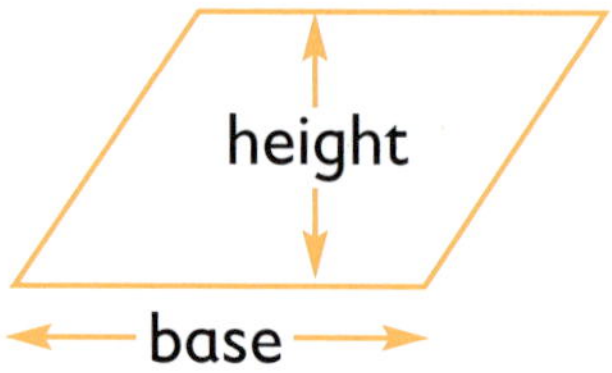

base × height

Trapezium

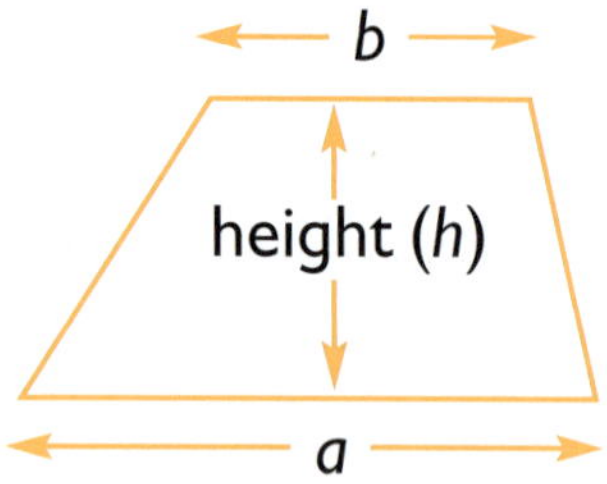

$\frac{(a + b)}{2} \times h$

LENGTH

Circle

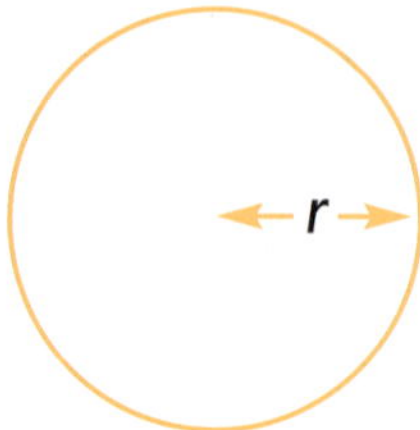

circumference = $2\pi r$

For a right-angled triangle

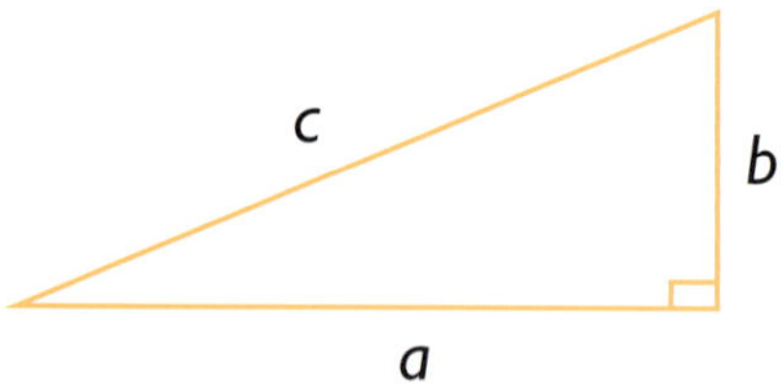

$a^2 + b^2 = c^2$ (Pythagoras' Theorem)

VOLUME

Prism

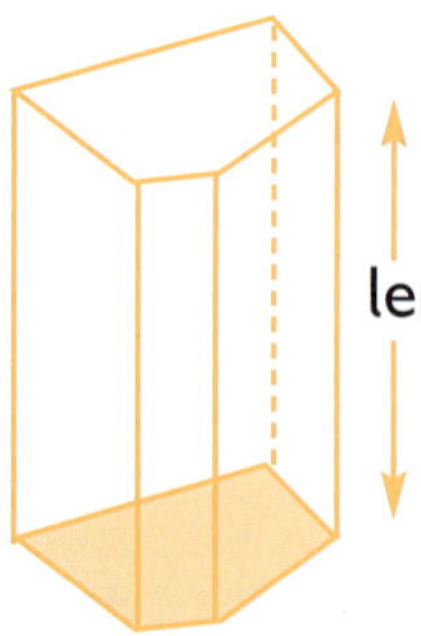

area of cross-section × length

You will need: pen, pencil, rubber, ruler, scientific or graphic calculator, a pair of compasses, tracing paper and a mirror (optional).

Perimeter problem

1 Shape A is a rectangle. Its **length** is **four times** its **width**.
Five of Shape A are joined together to make Shape B.

Shape A **Shape B**

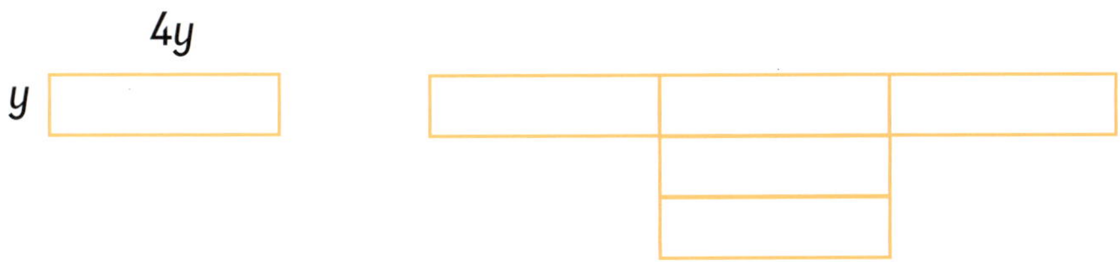

a Write an expression, using y, to show the **perimeter** of Shape A.
Give your answer in its simplest form.

_______ 1

b Write an expression, using y, to show the **perimeter** of Shape B.
Give your answer in its simplest form.

_______ 1

c If the perimeter of **Shape B** is **90 cm**, calculate the perimeter of Shape A in centimetres.

1

Perimeter of Shape A = _______________ cm

TOTAL 3

Goals

2 Chris and Sam play football for a local team.

Over the season, Chris scored **5** goals for every **3** goals that Sam scored.

a If **Chris** scored **35** goals, how many did **Sam** score?

1

b If **Sam** scored **18** goals, how many did **Chris** score?

1

c If they scored a **total** of **64** goals altogether, how many did they each score?

Chris scored ______________ Sam scored ______________

1

TOTAL

3

Approximating

3a The number of seabirds nesting on an offshore island has been recorded in a table.
The number of gannets nesting has been rounded to the nearest 100 and 1000.
Complete the table.

Birds	**Number nesting**	**Number to the nearest 100**	**Number to the nearest 1000**
Gannet	4782	4800	5000
Puffin	5360		
Cormorant	5538		

2

b The number of nesting razorbills is **4000** when rounded to the nearest 1000 and is **4300** when rounded to the nearest 100.
Write a number to show how many razorbills could nest on the island.

1

c The number of nesting gulls is **1000** when rounded to the nearest 1000 and **1500** when rounded to the nearest 100.
Give the **largest** and **smallest** number of gulls that could nest on the island.

Largest ______________ Smallest ______________

1

TOTAL

4

Cubes

4 Danny has a shape made from 5 small cubes. One cube is white; the rest are coloured.

Danny decides to add one more coloured cube to his shape. Here is a picture of one shape he could make.

a Sketch a picture of a different shape he could make. Shade the coloured cubes on your picture.

2

TOTAL

2

b Danny looks closely at this shape from six different angles. He looks from **above**, from **all four sides** and from **below**.
He draws the view from each angle.

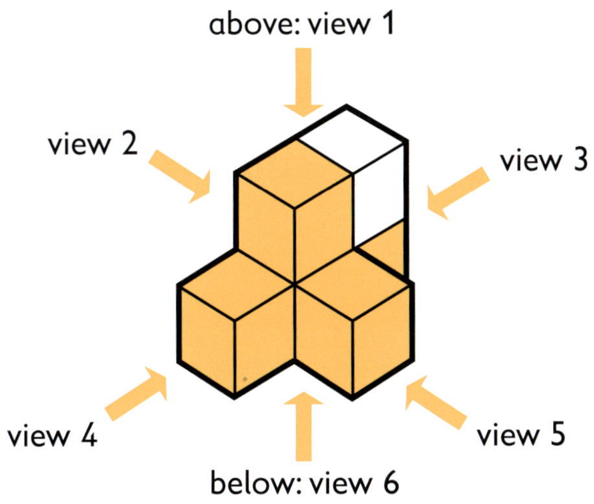

Danny's drawings are not in order. Write the number next to each drawing to show which view each is.
One has been done for you.

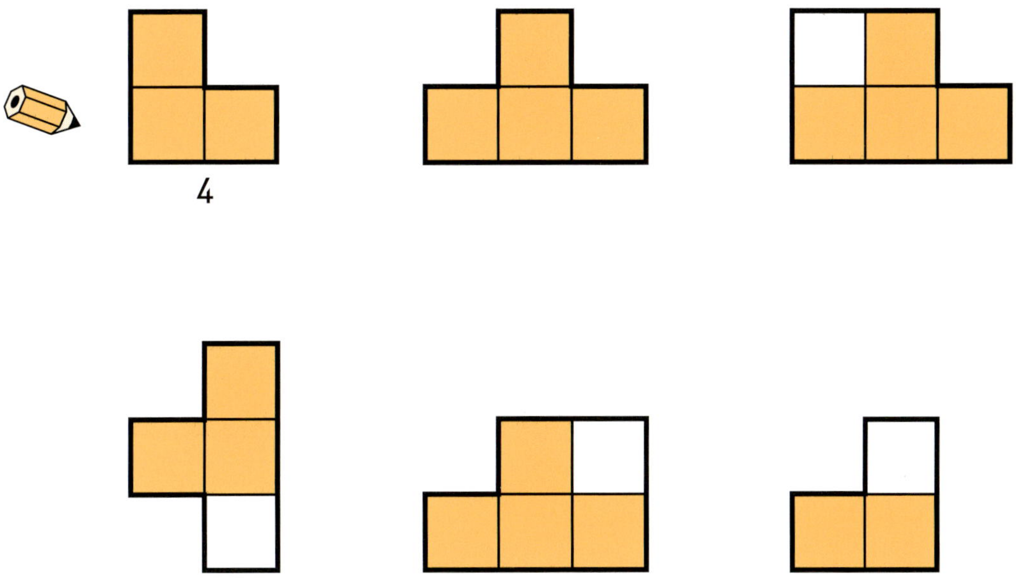

2

TOTAL

2

Expressions

5 Four boxes contain different expressions.

Box 1	Box 2	Box 3	Box 4
$p + q$	$2q + 1$	$4p + 7$	$q + 3p$

The expressions in **Box 1 and Box 2** can be **added** to make

$$p + 3q + 1$$

a Write an expression by adding **Box 3 and Box 4**.
Give your expression in its simplest form.

1

b Write an expression by adding together **all four** boxes.
Give your expression in its simplest form.

1

c Explain why the total of **all four** boxes (your answer to part b) must always be an **even** number.

1

TOTAL

3

Foreign exchange

6 The exchange rates for different countries are shown below.

£1 = 10.20 French Francs
£1 = 255 Spanish Pesetas

a Use the exchange rates above to find how much 35p is in French Francs.
You must show your working.

35p = ... French Francs

2

b Use the exchange rates above to find how much 867 Spanish Pesetas are in pounds. You must show your working.

867 Spanish Pesetas = £.............

2

c Use the exchange rates above to find how much 1 French Franc is in Spanish Pesetas. You must show your working.

1 French Franc = ... Spanish Pesetas

2

TOTAL

6

Area and volume

7 The diagonals of a square are 6.8 cm.

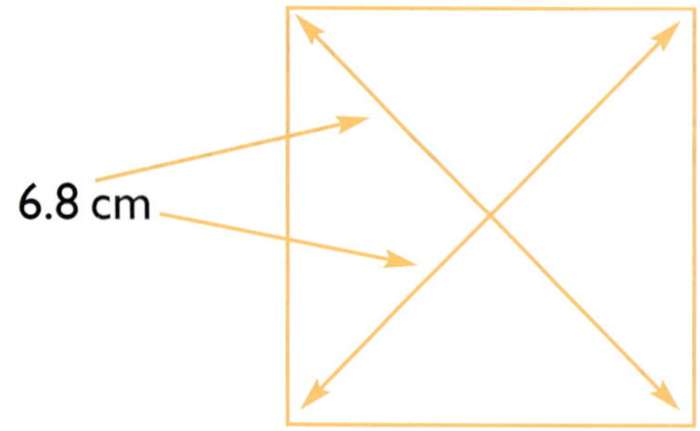

a Calculate the **area** of this square.
You will <u>not</u> get a mark for answering this question by drawing an accurate diagram. Show your working.

Area of square = ... cm^2

2

b The square is cut in half along one of its diagonals to make a triangle. This triangle is identical to the end face of a triangular prism which has a length of 8 cm.

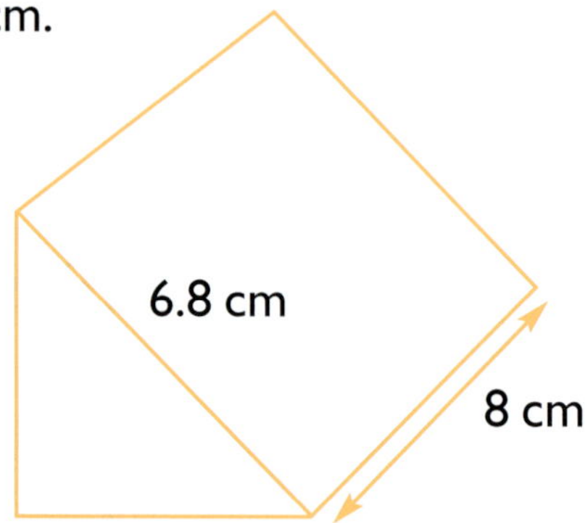

Calculate the volume of this triangular prism.
Show your working.

Volume of triangular prism = ... cm^3

2

TOTAL

4

Letters

8 In this puzzle, the letters x and y stand for numbers.
The totals for each row and column are given.

y	x	y	x	30 → y + x + y + x = 30
x	y	x	x	29
y	y	x	y	31
y	x	x	y	30
31	30	29	30	

Using the puzzle, write two equations and use them to find the values of the letters x and y.
Show your working.

x = ...   y = ...

3

TOTAL

3

Lawn problems

9 This diagram shows an aerial view of a rectangular lawn with a semi-circular pond.

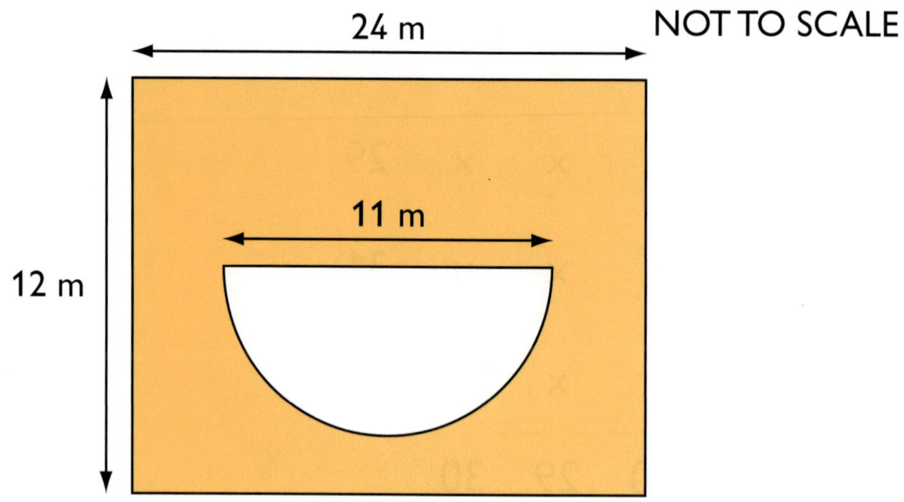

The **diameter** of the pond is **11 m**. The lawn has a length of **24 m** and a width of **12 m**.

a Find the area of the lawn (the shaded part in the diagram). Show your working. Take π to be 3.14. Give your answer to 2 decimal places.

.... m^2

3

TOTAL

3

A fence is built around the outside of the curved edge of the pond.
The fence is exactly **50 cm** from the edge.

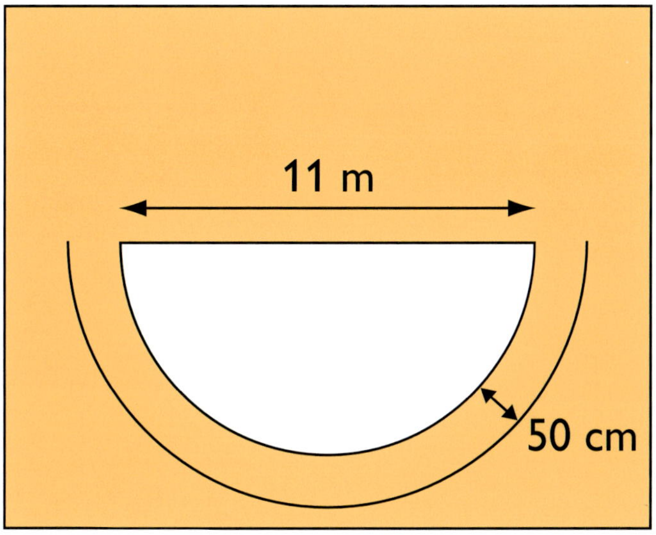

b Calculate the difference in length between the fence and the curved edge of the pond.
Give your answer to 2 decimal places.

.... m

2

c The pond has a depth of 1 m. Find the volume of water in the pond.
Give your answer in metres cubed (m^3) to 1 decimal place.

2

TOTAL

4

Travel

10 This simplified graph shows the journey of a car travelling from Leeds to Exeter, via Birmingham.

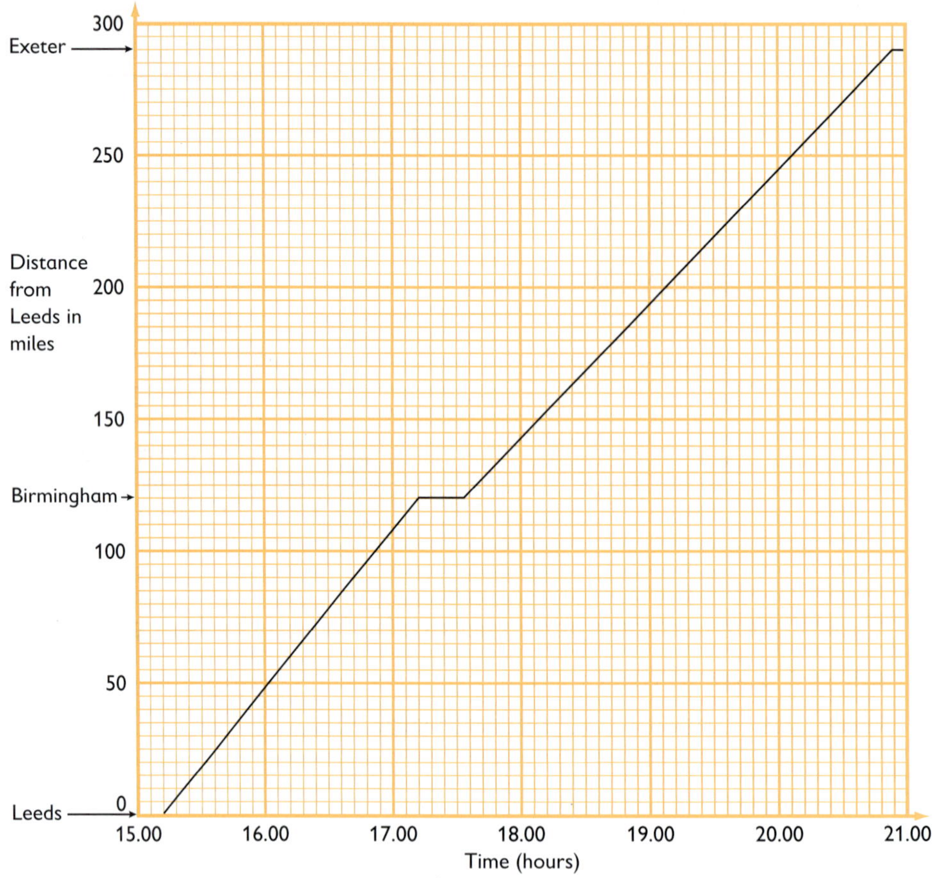

a Find the car's average speed between Leeds and Birmingham.

.... mph

1

TOTAL

1

b Look at the graph. Without calculating, say whether you think the average speed between Birmingham and Exeter is **greater** or **less** than the average speed between Leeds and Birmingham. Explain your answer.

1

c A second car is on a journey. It travels directly from **Exeter** to **Leeds**. The car leaves Exeter at 15.00 and travels at an average of 50 miles per hour (mph).
Calculate the time the car arrives in Leeds.

2

d Draw a line on the graph to show the second car's journey.
At one point on their journeys the two cars are the same distance from Leeds. What is this distance?

.... miles

1

TOTAL

4

Significant figures

11

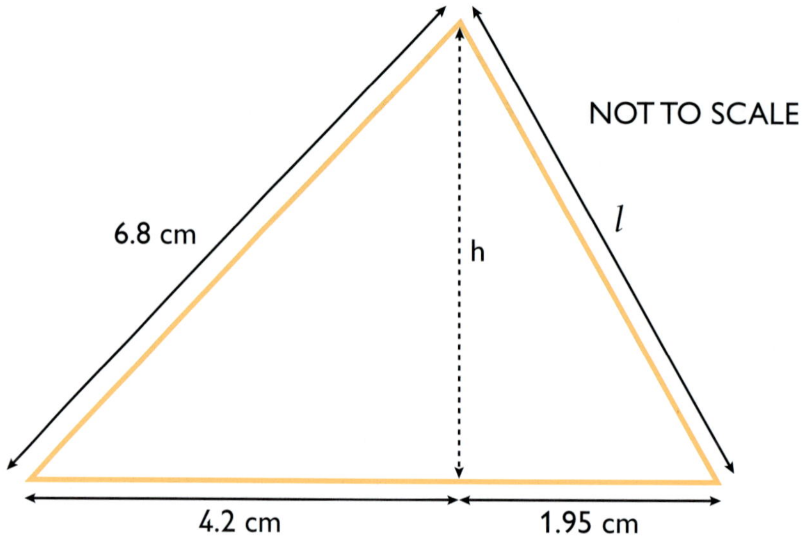

a Find the perpendicular height (h) of this triangle.
Give your answer to 3 significant figures.

2

b Use your answer to part (a) to find the length of side l.
Give your answer to 3 significant figures.

1

TOTAL

3

"For this first set of questions you have five seconds to work out each answer and write it down."

1 Write the number twenty thousand and two in figures.
2 One quarter of a number is eight and a half. What is the number?
3 How many grams are there in three kilograms?
4 There are four red balls and six blue balls in a bag. If I pick a ball at random, what is the probability that I pick a blue ball?
5 Write thirty per cent as a decimal.
6 Change the expression on the answer sheet into its simplest form.

"For the next set of questions you have ten seconds to work out each answer and write it down."

7 If your heart beats sixty times in one minute, how many times will it beat in one hour?
8 What percentage is four out of five?
9 Look at the answer sheet. What is the volume of the cube?
10 Write a fraction that is equivalent to two thirds.
11 Look at the answer sheet. If *s* equals seven, what does *t* equal?
12 What number must be added to nine point two to make twelve point one?
13 The value of eight *a* plus four *b* is thirty two. What is the value of four *a* plus two *b*?
14 Look at the answer sheet. What is the answer to the calculation?
15 Multiply twenty five by twenty three.
16 Look at the answer sheet. Use the calculation given to find the answer to four hundred and twelve multiplied by nine.
17 *a* stands for a number. Write an expression that means 'subtract three from *a* and then multiply the result by two'.
18 Look at the answer sheet. The pie chart shows how a garden centre divides its sales area. Approximately what percentage is used to sell flowers?

"For the next set of questions you have fifteen seconds to work out each answer and write it down."

19 What is nineteen multiplied by eight?

20 Look at the answer sheet. Angle *a* is forty degrees. What is the size of angle *b*?

21 Look at the answer sheet. If *x* equals six, what does *y* equal?

22 Look at the answer sheet. Draw a ring around the number that is a factor of two hundred and eighty seven.

23 Twenty eight out of seventy coach passengers were adults. What percentage were adults?

24 Look at the answer sheet. What is the approximate circumference of the circle?

25 Twenty four inches is about sixty centimetres. About how many centimetres is eighteen inches?

26 Look at the answer sheet. The cost of three items is shown. If you bought all three, what would be your change from three pounds?

27 Look at the answer sheet. Use the calculation given to help you find the answer to two point seven squared.

28 Look at the answer sheet. What is the size of angle *d*?

29 What is ninety divided by nought point five?

30 Divide thirty three pounds equally between six people. How much does each get?

5-second questions

1			1
2		$8\frac{1}{2}$	1
3	g		1
4			1
5		30%	1
6		$y + y - c$	1

10-second questions

7			1
8	%		1
9	cm^3	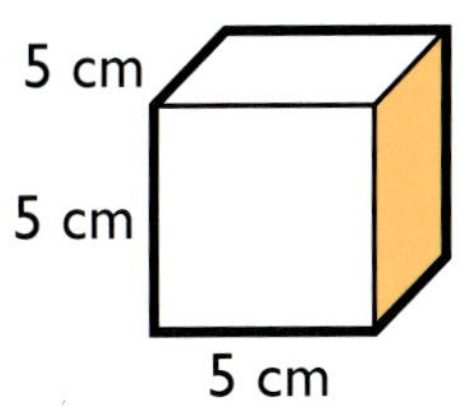	1
10		$\frac{2}{3}$	1

TOTAL

10

11 ________ $5s = t$ — 1

12 ________ 9.2 12.1 — 1

13 ________ $8a + 4b$ $4a + 2b$ — 1

14 ________ $12 + (8.2 - 5.9)$ — 1

15 ________ — 1

16 ________ $412 \times 8 = 3296$ — 1

17 ________ — 1

18 ________ — 1

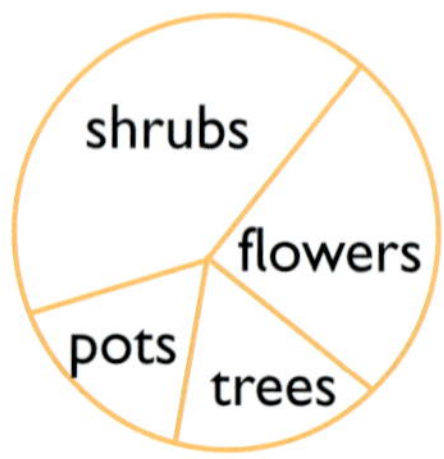

15-second questions

10 ________ — 1

20 $b =$ ° — 1

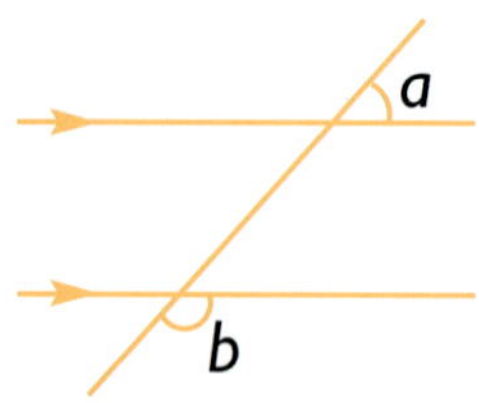

TOTAL

10

21 $y =$ | $y^2 = 2x + 4$ | 1

22 7 8 9 | 1

23 % | 1

24 m | 1

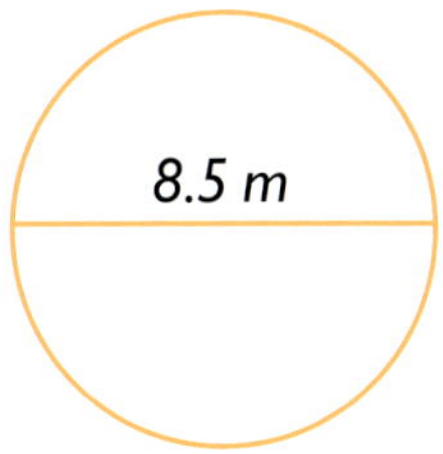

25 cm | 1

26 | 47p £1.53 82p | 1

27 | $27^2 = 729$ | 1

28 $d =$ ° | 1

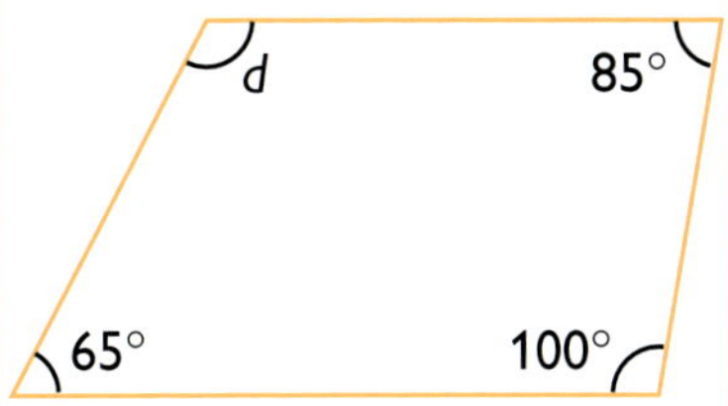

29 | 1

30 | 1

TOTAL

10

Maths Test Answers

Paper 1

Question number	Answer	Mark	Comments and tips
Practice questions	$\frac{7}{8}$ $\frac{1}{4}$	0	You cannot use calculators for *any* of the questions in Paper 1. You can work answers out anywhere on the page or you can work answers out mentally. For some questions you might gain a mark for your written working out even if you get the answer wrong.
Fractions and percentages			
1a	$\frac{7}{10}$	1	Seven out of ten pieces of chocolate have been eaten.
1b	$\frac{2}{5}$ 60%	1 1	Four out of ten pieces of chocolate have been eaten. $\frac{4}{10}$ is the same value as $\frac{2}{5}$ Six out of ten pieces have not been eaten. $\frac{6}{10}$ is the same value as $\frac{60}{100}$ which is 60%.
1c	Two of the squares should be shaded.	1	$\frac{2}{12}$ is the same value as $\frac{1}{6}$
1d	Fourteen of the squares should be shaded.	1	70% is the same value as $\frac{70}{100}$ which is $\frac{7}{10}$ This means that for every ten squares seven should be shaded, totalling fourteen out of twenty.
Co-ordinates			
2a	(2,1) (3,3) (5,3) (6,2) These sets of co-ordinates can be in any order.	1	Remember that the *x* co-ordinate is the first co-ordinate and tells you how many across to travel from 0. The *y* co-ordinate comes second and tells you how many up to travel from 0. (2, 1) means across 2 and up 1.
2b	(2,5) (3,7) (5,7) (6,6) (in any order)	1	Remember that the *x* co-ordinate is the first co-ordinate and tells you how many across to travel from 0. The phrase '*x* is a cross, *x* is across' can help you to remember.
2c	Shape B is the same as Shape A but has been moved (translated) up four places.	1	If you add something to all the *y* co-ordinates the shape appears to move up. If you subtract from all the *y* co-ordinates it appears to move down.
2d	The shape will appear to move across two places to the left.	1	If you add something to all the *x* co-ordinates the shape appears to move to the right. If you subtract from all the *x* co-ordinates the shape appears to move to the left.

Question number	Answer	Mark	Comments and tips
Missing numbers			
3(a – e)	8 10 113 40 72 1 mark for each	5	Always look at the finished equation when you have written a missing number to see if it makes sense. For the question ☐ – 40 = 73, if you <u>incorrectly</u> subtracted 40 from 73 and wrote the missing number 33, you can see that 33 –40 doesn't equal 73!
Multiplying			
4	20 7 10 200 70 270 5 100 35 135 405	3	If most of the diagram is correct but the final answer is incorrect you get two marks.
Milk			
5a	$\frac{1}{6}$	1	There are 24 bottles. The probability of picking a skimmed bottle is 4 out of 24. $\frac{4}{24}$ is the same value as $\frac{1}{6}$
5b	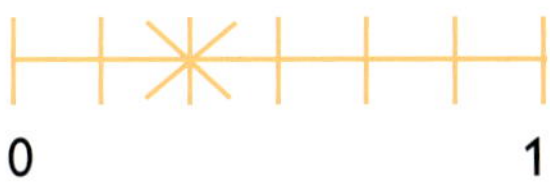	1	There are 24 bottles. The probability of picking full-cream is 8 out of 24. $\frac{8}{24}$ is the same value as $\frac{2}{6}$ or $\frac{1}{3}$ Note that $\frac{1}{6}$ can be marked on the line by splitting the whole line into 6 equal parts.
5c		1	The probability of picking full-cream is 8 out of 24, so the probability of not picking one is 16 out of 24. $\frac{16}{24}$ is the same value as $\frac{4}{6}$ or $\frac{2}{3}$
5d	The third statement only should be ticked.	1	There are still 11 half-fat bottles out of the 23 left. $\frac{11}{23}$ is greater than $\frac{8}{23}$ (full-cream) or $\frac{4}{23}$ (skimmed)
Rainfall			
6a	False False True ✓ False	2	1 mark if one answer is incorrect.
6b	4.5 cm	1	The range can be found by subtracting the lowest value from the highest, i.e. 4.5 – 0
6c	March 8th's bar should be drawn in to the value of 4.5 cm	1	The mean value (4 cm) is the total of all the values divided by 7 (the number of days).
6d	3 cm	1	The mean value of the first week is 2 cm. This can be found by adding all the values to get 14 cm and dividing by 7 (the number of days). The second week has a mean of 4 cm, so the mean over the whole period is 3 cm.

Question number	Answer	Mark	Comments and tips
Negatives			
7a	3	1	Imagine a number line, e.g. −5 −4 −3 −2 −1 0 1 2 3 4 5 Starting at −5 you need to count on 3 to reach the number −2.
7b	9	1	
7c	6	1	
7d	$^{-}3 + 8 - 2$ or $8 + {}^{-}3 - 2$ or $8 - 2 + {}^{-}3$ or $^{-}3 - 2 + 8$	1	Watch out for subtracting negative numbers, e.g. $8 - {}^{-}3$ as this will actually result in the answer 11, the same as 8 + 3.
Equations			
8a	$a = 6$ $b = 8$ $c = 4$ 1 mark each	3	$2a + 7 = 19$, so $2a = 19 - 7 = 12$ If $2a = 12$, then a must be 6. $5b - 16 = 24$, so $5b = 24 + 16 = 40$ If $5b = 40$, then b must be 8. $2c^2 + 5 = 37$, so $2c^2 = 37 - 5 = 32$ If $2c^2 = 32$, then $c^2 = 16$ and c must be 4.
8b	l = 27 cm 1 mark for showing the expression 4l – 16 in your working.	2	The perimeter is the distance all the way around the edge of the shape. The perimeter therefore is l + l – 8 + l + l – 8 = 4l – 16. So 92 cm (the perimeter given) = 4L – 16 4L – 16 = 92, so 4L = 92 + 16 = 108. If 4L = 108, l must be 27.
Fractions			
9a	$\frac{1}{8}$ 9 $\frac{9}{32}$ 19 $\frac{19}{32}$ 24 $\frac{3}{4}$ 8	5	1 mark given for each correct fraction. 1 mark given for the other numbers correct.
Sequences			
10a	13	1	
10b	5 7 19 All three numbers must be correct.	1	You will see that the number of squares in a layer is always two more than twice the layer number.
10c	$2n - 1$ or $(2 \times n) - 1$	1	
10c	n^2	2	If you look at the number of squares altogether in a model with 2 layers you can see it is 4. If you look at a model with 3 layers you will see it has 9 squares. If you look at a model with 4 layers you will see it has 16 squares. From this you can generalise that when there are n layers there must be n^2 squares.

Maths Test Answers

Paper 2

Question number	Answer	Mark	Comments and tips
Perimeter problem			
1a	$10y$	1	The perimeter of a shape is the distance all the way around the edge. Here the perimeter is $y + 4y + y + 4y = 10y$.
1b	$30y$	1	The perimeter of a shape is the distance all the way around the edge. Here the perimeter is 6 short sides ($y \times 6$) plus four longer sides ($4y \times 4$) which equals $30y$ in total.
1c	30 cm	1	If the perimeter of the larger shape ($30y$) is 90 cm, divide 90 by 30 to find y. $90 \div 30 = 3$, therefore $y = 3$. To find the perimeter of shape A ($10y$) we know that $y = 3$, so $10y = 30$.
Goals			
2a	21	1	Chris scored 5 for every 3 goals that Sam scored. We can write this as the ratio 5:3. If Chris scored 35 (seven times his number in the ratio) then Sam must have scored seven times his number in the ratio, i.e. $7 \times 3 = 21$.
2b	30	1	Using the ratio 5:3, if Sam scored 18 (six times his number in the ratio) then Chris must have scored six times his number in the ratio, i.e. $6 \times 5 = 30$.
2c	40 and 24	1	In the ratio 5:3, there are a total of 8 parts. If a total of 64 goals are scored (eight times the ratio total) then Chris and Sam both must have scored eight times their numbers in the ratio.
Bird count			
3a	5400 5000 5500 6000 1 mark for each correct row	2	
3b	A number between 4250 and 4349.	1	Numbers ending in 5, 50 and 500 are rounded up rather than down when rounded to the nearest 10, 100 and 1000 respectively.
3c	Largest = 1499 Smallest = 1450	1	If the number was above 1499, i.e. 1500, it would round to 2000, to the nearest 1000. If the number was below 1450, i.e. 1449 it would round to 1400 to the nearest 100.
Cubes			
4a	An accurate drawing of the shape with an extra coloured cube. Only one cube should be left unshaded.	2	The coloured cubes must be shaded to get both marks.
4b	4 6 2 1 5 3 1 mark only if two are incorrect.	2	

Question number	Answer	Mark	Comments and tips
Expressions			
5a	$7p + q + 7$	1	For the expression to be in its simplest form the like terms should be collected.
5b	$8p + 4q + 8$	1	
5c	Your explanation should show how you can tell that the expression is even, preferably by showing that $2(4p + 2q + 4)$ is the same as the expression.	1	Be careful not to just repeat the question in your answer, e.g. by saying "It is even" without proving it. If a number is even it is a multiple of 2 and we can see this is a multiple of 2 by factorising, creating the expression $2(4p + 2q + 4)$.
Exchange rates			
6a	3.57	2	Divide 10.2 French Francs by 100 to find how many Francs are the same as 1 pence. Then multiply by 35.
6b	£3.40 You do not get an answer for writing 3.4 or £3.4.	2	Divide 867 Pesetas by 255 to find how many pounds they are equivalent to.
6c	25	2	Divide 255 Spanish Pesetas by 10.2 to find how many Pesetas are equivalent to one Franc.
Area and volume			
7a	$23.12\ cm^2$	2	There are several ways of answering this question. The simplest way is to look at the square as four right-angled triangles. The four triangles must have perpendicular sides of 3.4 (half 6.8) and so the area of one triangle is $\frac{1}{2} \times 3.4 \times 3.4$. Multiply this answer by 4 to find the area of the square. A second method (if confident) is to use Pythagoras' Theorem ($a^2 + b^2 = c^2$) for one of these triangles. This can help you to find the length of one side of the square or, better still, this length squared (the area) e.g. $3.4^2 + 3.4^2 = c^2$... c^2 is the same as the area as c is one side of the square.
7b	$92.48\ cm^3$ If your answer to part (a) is wrong you can get 1 mark if you have worked out this answer by dividing your answer to part (a) by 2 and multiplying by 8.	2	To find the volume, multiply the area of the end face by the length, i.e. area of triangle = half the area of the square (part a) × 10: $23.12 \div 2 \times 10$.
Letters			
8	$x = 7$ $y = 8$ 1 mark for two of these equations shown: $2x + 2y = 30$ $3x + y = 29$ $3y + x = 31$ 2 marks for getting the answer to either x or y (but not both) correct.	3	There are different methods for solving simultaneous equations, including the substitution method of which an example is shown below: Halve each value in $2x + 2y = 30$ to give the equation $x + y = 15$ $x + y = 15$ therefore $y = 15 - x$ Substitute $15 - x$ for y in the equation $3x + y = 29$ $3x + (15 - x) = 29$, therefore $2x + 15 = 29$, and $2x = 14$, so x must equal 7. This can be inserted into the equation $x + y = 15$, to show that $y = 8$.

Question number	Answer	Mark	Comments and tips
Lawn problems			
9a	240.51 m^2 2 marks if your answer is not rounded to 2 decimal places. 1 mark if you have correctly found the area of the semi-circle as 47.4925 m^2. Only 2 marks given for 240.48 m^2 (use of π button on calculator)	3	To find the area of the lawn first find the area of the pond: Area of a circle = πr^2 ($\div$ 2 as it is a semi-circle) Area of pond = $\pi \times 5.5^2 \div 2 = 47.4925$ m^2 Subtract this from the area of the rectangle ($12 \times 24 = 288$ m^2) $288 - 47.4925 = 240.5075$ m^2 NOTE: *If you have used the π button on your calculator your answers will be different. The question stated that π should be taken as 3.14.*
9b	1.57 m 1 mark for the answer 3.14 (twice the correct answer).	2	Circumference = $2\pi r$ or πd Length of curved edge of semi-circle = $11 \times \pi \div 2$ Length of fence = $12 \times \pi \div 2$ The difference is found by subtracting one from the other.
9c	47.5 m^3 1 mark if your answer is the same number as given for the area of the pond calculated in part (a), but given in m^3.	2	The volume is depth multiplied by the area of the surface, i.e. the area of the semi-circle.
Travel			
10a	60 mph	1	The car travels 120 miles in two hours, so 60 miles in one hour.
10b	Your answer must show that you've noticed that the gradient (slope) is steeper for the first part of the graph so the average speed between Birmingham and Exeter must be less than between Leeds and Birmingham.	1	The steeper the gradient, the faster the speed; in other words, the car travels more miles in a shorter time.
10c	20.48 1 mark for the number 5.8 in your working.	2	It would take the car 5.8 hours. This is found by dividing 290 miles by 50 mph. 0.8 hours is 48 minutes. This can be found by multiplying $0.8 \times 60 = 48$. So the journey would take 5 hours and 48 minutes.
10d	140 miles	1	The point where your two lines should cross.
Significant figures			
11a	5.35 cm 1 mark if your answer has more than 3 digits, e.g. 5.34789 or 5.347	2	Use Pythagoras' Theorem ($a^2 + b^2 = c^2$). $4.2^2 + h^2 = 6.8^2$ so $h^2 = 6.8^2 - 4.2^2$ $h^2 = 28.6$, therefore $h = 5.347897$ cm
11b	5.69 cm 1 mark if your answer has more than 3 digits, e.g. 5.69429	1	Use your answer to part (a) and Pythagoras' Theorem ($a^2 + b^2 = c^2$). $1.95^2 + 5.35^2 = l^2$ $l^2 = 32.425$, therefore $l = 5.69$ cm.

Mental Maths Test

Answers

1. 20002
2. 34
3. 3000 g
4. $\frac{3}{5}$ or equivalent e.g. $\frac{6}{10}$
5. 0.3
6. $2y - c$
7. 3600
8. 80%
9. 125 cm^3
10. any fraction equivalent to $\frac{2}{3}$ e.g. $\frac{4}{6}$
11. 35
12. 2.9
13. 16
14. 14.3
15. 575
16. 3708
17. $2(a-3)$
18. approx. 25%
19. 152
20. 140°
21. 4
22. 7
23. 40%
24. approx. 26 cm
25. 45 cm
26. 18p
27. 7.29
28. 110°
29. 180
30. £5.50

National Curriculum Levels

Write your scores below.

Mark scored in Paper 1		out of 45
Mark scored in Paper 2		out of 45
Mark scored in Mental Test		out of 30
Total score		out of 120

Use this table to find what level you might be working at.

Mark	0 – 16	17 – 32	33 – 65	66 – 100	101 – 110	111 – 120
Level	**Level 3**	**Level 4**	**Level 5**	**Level 6**	**Level 7**	**Level 8**

English at Key Stage 3

In English pupils are required to sit two test papers.

Paper 1

Time allowed: 1 hour 30 minutes plus 15 minutes reading time

Section A – a test of reading based on a narrative or descriptive piece.

Section B – a test of reading based on an information text or on a poem.

Section C – a test of writing. Several options are given: writing a story, writing an argument or expressing a personal point of view.

Paper 2

Time allowed: 1 hour 15 minutes

This is based on the study of a Shakespeare play at Key Stage 3. For 2001 the choices are **Henry V, Twelfth Nigh**t and **Macbeth**.

A booklet containing printed versions of scenes from the play is provided. A copy of the entire text is not permitted in the test.

Two questions are set on different scenes and each pupil must choose one of these for which to supply an answer.

Marking the papers

Paper 1

Section A is marked simply for the understanding of the passage set. This is judged by reading and writing tasks although the way in which the answers are written is not assessed.

Section B is marked for the ability to understand and describe the author's intention – how the author intended to influence the reader. Again, this is judged by reading and writing tasks although the way in which the answers are written is not assessed.

Section C is marked for the ability to write and communicate ideas. The style of writing does matter here as do the quality of ideas and grammatical features such as sentence structure, spelling, punctuation and grammar.

The mark scheme will vary from year to year for this paper but it will generally be worth about 60 marks.

Paper 2

This paper on a Shakespeare play is marked for:

- Understanding and response – an understanding of Shakespeare's meaning and intention.
- Written expression – an ability to write clearly using grammatical features such as sentence structure, spelling, punctuation and grammar.

The mark scheme varies from year to year for this paper but it will generally be worth about 40 marks.

Tips for success at Key Stage 3

- Look at the entire test paper first to establish what has to be done. Highlight the time restraints and the number of questions which need to be answered.
- Pace yourself – keep an eye on the clock.
- Read the questions carefully. Underline key words, e.g. 'compare', 'two reasons'. Be relevant in your answers.
- Avoid getting too involved with any one question. You may have a great deal to say about it, but it will only be worth a set number of marks.
- Follow the help given on the paper. If the examiners have given a list of points to follow then use these as the plan for your work.
- Make notes on the test paper. Underline important points and circle or highlight information relevant to the question.
- Back up points you make with short quotations from the passage.
- If you get stuck on a question, leave it for the moment – but remember to leave a page empty in your answer book in case you want to go back.
- Your basic English is important – you need to communicate what you know and understand. Look carefully for those words you always spell incorrectly!
- If you have time left, go back over your answers.

Advice for parents

The tests in this book are modelled as closely as possible on the 'real thing' so pupils will not be surprised by the test format. However, parents can help with the pressure of the tests by using the material in this book as a resource for teaching and learning. Do not just sit a pupil down with the test and tell him or her to 'get on with it'; share the experiences, questions and discussion that arise from the tests. Try sitting one yourself!

- Talk about each of the questions and possible ways forward.
- Choose a comfortable, secure environment in which to do the tests.
- Mark the work together, praising positive points as well as pointing out things which are not correct.
- Look closely at how the incorrect responses can be corrected, what needs to be learned or changed and how this can be done realistically. It is useful to list just two or three things which need to be learned before the next test session.
- Stick to the time limits – but do not insist that the entire test paper has to be completed at one go.
- Give immediate feedback – do not wait too long to discuss performance.
- Be positive about achievements!

- At the beginning of this test, you have 15 minutes to read the paper and make notes but you must not start to write your answers until you are told.
- Then you have 1 hour and 30 minutes to write your answers.
- You should answer ALL the questions in Sections A and B.
- Then choose ONE question only from Section C.
- You should spend about: 20 minutes on question 1
  10 minutes on question 2
  20 minutes on question 3
  35 minutes on question 4
  5 minutes checking your work.
- Check your work carefully.

N.B.

Don't be afraid to underline, circle or highlight the key points in the texts as you are reading them. You can write in the margin of the pages, too.

Read the following passage.

Then answer question 1 and question 2.

The passage comes from ***London Labour and the London Poor****, a collection of interviews written by a journalist in nineteenth-century London. It tells you how young people of the time celebrated the Guy Fawkes tradition every November 5*th.

I always go out with a Guy Fawkes every year. I'm seventeen years old and I've done this every year I can remember, except last year. My father was an undertaker; he's been dead four months. He didn't like me going out on Guy Fawkes. He didn't like it at all. Said it was a disgrace.

I couldn't have been more than seven years old when I first began. They put paper hangings round my legs – sometimes they bought, and sometimes they got given them; but they gave a rare lot for a penny or twopence. After that they put me in an apron made of some sort of paper – showy, you know – and they put a lot of tinsel bows, and at the corners they cut a sort of tail… it looked stunnin'; then they put on my chest a tinsel heart and rosettes; they were green and red because it shows off. All up my arms I had bows and things to make a showoff. Then I put on a black mask with a little red on the cheek to make me look like a devil: it had horns, too. Always pick out a devil's mask with horns: it looks fine and frightens people most. The boy that dressed me was a very clever chap, and made a guy to rights. Why, he made me a little guy about a foot high, to carry in my lap – it was pieces of quilting, like, a sort of patch-work all sewn together – and then filled it with sawdust and made a head of shavings. He picked the shavings small, and then sewed them up in a little bag; and then he painted a face, and it looked very well; and he made it a little tinsel bob-tail coat and a tinsel cap with two feathers on the top. It was made to sit in a chair, and there was a piece of string tied to each of the legs and the arms; and a string came behind; and I used to pull it and the legs and arms jumped up.

I was put in a chair and two old broom-handles were put through the rails, and then a boy got in front and another behind; and carried me off round Holborn way in the streets and the squares. Every now and then they put me down before a window, then one of 'em used to say the speech and I used all the time to keep pulling the string of my little guy and it amused the children in the windows. After they'd said the speech some of them went and knocked on the door and asked 'Please to remember the guy' and the little children brought ha'pence and pence; sometimes the ladies and gentlemen chucked money out of the window. At last they carried me to Russell Square. They put me down before a gentleman's house and began saying the speech. While they were saying it, up comes a lot of boys with sticks in their hands. One of our chaps knew what they were after, and took the little guy out of my hand and went on saying the speech. I kept on sitting still.

After a bit one of these boys says, 'Oh, it's a dead guy; let's have a lark with it!' and then one of them gives me a punch with his fist and then snatched the mask off my face, and when he pulled it off he says, 'Oi, Bill, it's a live 'un!' We were afraid we should get the worst of it so we ran away round the Square. The biggest boy of the lot carried the chair. After we'd run a little way they caught us again and says, 'Now then, give us all your money.' With that some ladies and gentlemen that saw it all came up and says, 'If you don't go, we'll lock you up,' and so they let us go away.

Then they asked me to be guy again, but I wouldn't for I'd got a black eye through it already. So they got another to finish the day. When we got home that night we shared two shillings apiece. There were five of us altogether; but I think they chiselled me. I know they got a deal more than that, for they had a good many sixpences and shillings.

Question 1 10 marks in total

Imagine you were going to be a guy as described in this passage.

a) Make a list of all the things you would need.

b) Write a set of instructions about how to make the guy.

In your answer you should concentrate on:

- Making a numbered list of the essential elements.
- Writing these in your own words.
- Writing your instructions in the correct order.
- Using the correct verb forms, e.g. 'Take a…'.
- Linking your instructions with appropriate connectives, e.g. 'after this… then…'.

Refer to words or phrases in the passage to support your ideas.

Question 2 8 marks in total

Explain how this passage gives you a sense of the character of the speaker.

In your answer you should comment on:

- His use of informal language.
- What happens to the boy and how he expresses his feelings about it.
- His reactions to people and events.

Refer to words or phrases in the passage to support your ideas.

Read the poem below.
Then answer question 3.

The poem is about how the events of the Guy Fawkes celebrations bring back memories to the poet.

Gunpowder Plot

For days these curious cardboard buds have lain
In brightly coloured boxes. Soon the night
Will come. We pray there'll be no sullen* rain
To make these magic orchids flame less bright.

Now in the garden's darkness they begin
To flower: the frenzied whizz of Catherine wheel
Puts forth its fiery petals and the thin
Rocket soars to burst upon the steel

Bulwark** of a cloud. And then the guy,
Absurdly human phoenix***, is again
Gulped by greedy flames: the harvest sky
Is flecked with threshed and glittering golden grain.

'Uncle! A cannon! Watch me as I light it!'
The women helter-skelter, squealing high,
Retreat; the paper fuse is quickly lit,
A cat-like hiss, and spit of fire, a sly

Falter, and then the air is shocked with blast.
The cannon bangs and in my nostrils drifts
A bitter scent that brings the lurking past
Lurching to my side. The present shifts,

Allows a ten-year old memory to walk
Unhindered now; and so I'm forced to hear
The banshee**** howl of mortar and the talk
Of men who died, am forced to taste my fear.

I listen for a moment to the guns,
The torn earth's grunts, recalling how I prayed.
The past retreats. I hear a corpse's sons –
'Who's scared of bangers!' 'Uncle! John's afraid!'

Vernon Scannell

* miserable or gloomy
** a solid, wall-like structure built for defence
*** a mythical creature which died in fire but rose again in the ashes
**** a frightening ghost

Question 3 10 marks in total

a) How does the poet build up a picture of the fireworks party in the garden?

6 marks

In your answer you should comment on:

- How he describes the fireworks as they explode.
- How he describes the night and the garden.
- The reactions of people to the fireworks.
- Any other senses he appeals to in his imagery, e.g. smell.
- The comparisons he uses to create the pictures and atmosphere.

Refer to words and phrases in the poem to support your ideas.

b) Explain how the fireworks re-create an earlier memory.

4 marks

In your answer you should comment on:

- The starting point of the bad memory is 'cannon' – a kind of firework but also a gun used in war.
- The smells which conjure up the images and what they remind him of.
- How long ago the event happened to him.
- Other words connected with war.
- Who the children are with him at the fireworks party.

Refer to words and phrases in the poem to support your ideas.

English Test

Paper 1 Section C

This section of the paper is a test of writing. You will be assessed on:

- Your ideas and the way you organise them;
- Your ability to write clearly, using paragraphs and accurate grammar, spelling and punctuation.

Question 4 32 marks in total

Choose ONE of the following:

EITHER

a **Write an article for a magazine to be read in the USA, which explains how young people today celebrate Guy Fawkes Day on November 5th and how this compares to how it was celebrated in the past.**

In your answer you should:

- Use the appropriate style for a piece of journalism.
- Use comparison of then and now.
- Remember that your audience will not have heard of or understand the significance of this festival.

OR

b **Write an eye-witness account of a bonfire-night celebration you have attended, making it as atmospheric and detailed as possible.**

In your answer you could:

- Write about a real or a made-up event.
- Try to create the atmosphere of place in your description.
- Think about all the senses affected by fireworks.

OR

c **'Never fool with fireworks'. Imagine you read a letter in a local newspaper stating that fireworks are dangerous and should be banned. Write a letter in reply disagreeing with the author and explaining how fireworks are not dangerous if safety rules are followed.**

In your answer you should:

- Write in appropriate letter style.
- Make it clear you know what safety issues are involved and how they can be used effectively.
- Aim to persuade readers of your point of view.

Preparing for the Shakespeare test

There's only one way to prepare for answering questions on a Shakespeare play – read the play! Watching the video is not good enough!

In your test, you will be asked to deal with one aspect of the play you have studied in relation to one or two scenes, but you must also be prepared to share your knowledge of the rest of the play by putting certain aspects of the play into context and saying what has happened before – and if anything has changed – and even what will happen later in the play.

Remember: Do not write everything you know about the play – you are not being tested on how good your memory is. Answer the question you have been set – not the one you want to be set!

Draft your answer before you finally write it:

- Take time to think about what information you need from the scene printed for you.
- Spend at least 15 minutes reading the scene you have chosen carefully.
- Do not be afraid to underline or circle important quotations. Write notes in the margin as you go along.
- Use the helpful pointers given to you on the question paper and write notes on each section. Prove each of your points with a brief quotation.
- Take each of these pointers in turn and think about how to join them together as paragraphs later on. You could even number them in your notes, to ensure that you do not miss any out.
- Do not write out huge sections from the play. The examiner wants to know what and how you write – not how Shakespeare did!

It is important that you time yourself effectively. You need to pace yourself. You have time to read and annotate the scene printed for you and time to draft and write your answer. You will not be given extra time.

You are being assessed in this section on your knowledge and awareness of the Shakespeare play you have studied – its plot, ideas, the characters and why they behave in the way that they do, the language and even the staging of the scene. But remember, you will also have to write clearly to communicate these ideas. Hence marks are allocated for use of appropriate style, clarity and organisation of writing, spelling, grammar and punctuation. Your handwriting is also important, so leave enough time to check your work.

Checklist of important features in your answer

Features to consider
Paragraphs Is my work divided into paragraphs so that the examiner can see when I stop writing about one aspect and start writing about another? This is an important stylistic feature and helps you to communicate your message clearly.
Quotations Are my quotations too long? Have I used quotation marks? Have I started long quotations on a new line? Have I written my quotations on lines as in the text? Have I introduced my quotations by using a colon (:)?
Style Am I writing in an appropriate style? Is my writing too chatty? Have I written in complete sentences? Is my handwriting clear and neat?
Length The answer booklet you are given is A4 in size. Have I written between 3 and 4 sides on paper for my answer? If you use any pages for planning, draw a line through these notes.

Marking your tests

Your work on a Shakespeare play will be considered from two points of view:

- **Understanding and Response:** the content of what you write – how you have understood and responded to Shakespeare and his ideas, how his characters behave and why they do, the development and changes in the plot and his language.
- **Written Expression:** the way you write – your choice of appropriate style, your use of paragraphs, vocabulary, punctuation and spelling as well as your ability to write clearly and legibly.

There is not a 'perfect answer': everyone's response will be different but there are set criteria to help marking (see pages 71 and 75).

To achieve the highest grades you will need to:

- Know and understand your Shakespeare play well
- Write clearly and to the point – do not ramble on, giving irrelevant information from the play just because you know it
- Answer the question you have been set in an organised way
- Write from a personal point of view so the examiner gets a sense of what you think and feel – not just what your teacher said
- Write accurately in clear, well-punctuated English, using well-constructed sentences.

Henry V
If you have studied **Henry V** do this task.

Time allowed: 75 minutes

Your work will be assessed for your knowledge and understanding of the play and the way you express your ideas.

Check your work carefully.

Henry V
From Act 4 Scene 1
Task
The play is intensely patriotic and concerns itself with the development of a heroic king.
- Show how in this scene Shakespeare is able to give a very human and personal picture of Henry, and why this is important in the development of our perception of the king.

Before you write you should think about:
- What Henry was like as a young man.
- How he changed to become a responsible king in the first half of the play.
- How he dealt with the three traitors.
- What he has been like during the battles in France and how he has redeemed his reputation.
- Why he walks alone and disguised among his men before Agincourt.
- What his responses to the men and his soliloquies prove about him as a 'man'.
- How he takes forward the story with Williams later on in the play.

Read the task again before you begin to write your answer.

EXAMINER'S TIPS

Remind yourself about some of the following points:
- Set the scene in the context of the rest of the play. Henry was once seen as a tearaway – 'His hours filled up with riots, banquets, sports' – but when he became king he realised that he would have to take on responsibility – 'The king is full of grace and kind regard'.
- He deals with the three traitors Scroop, Cambridge and Grey cleverly and as a tactician.
- In France he leads his troops bravely at Harfleur, but by the time they need to challenge the French at Agincourt they are heavily outnumbered and tired.
- He disguises himself the night before Agincourt and discovers how his men really feel about him and the war. He reflects upon the nature of Kingship and its responsibility. We feel sympathy for him in this situation.
- He uses his feelings and his men's feelings about being victims to spur his men on to patriotism so that they win the battle of Agincourt.
- In this way we see how the 'man' Henry makes his way to become a famous king.

Henry V

From Act 4 Scene 1

KING HENRY V	… Every subject's duty is the king's; but every subject's soul is his own. Therefore should every soldier in the wars do as every sick man in his bed, wash every mote out of his conscience: and dying so, death is to him advantage; or not dying, the time was blessedly lost wherein such preparation was gained: and in him that escapes, it were not sin to think that, making God so free an offer, He let him outlive that day to see His greatness and to teach others how they should prepare.
WILLIAMS	'Tis certain, every man that dies ill, the ill upon his own head, the king is not to answer it.
BATES	But I do not desire he should answer for me; and yet I determine to fight lustily for him.
KING HENRY V	I myself heard the king say he would not be ransomed.
WILLIAMS	Ay, he said so, to make us fight cheerfully: but when our throats are cut, he may be ransomed, and we ne'er the wiser.
KING HENRY V	If I live to see it, I will never trust his word after.
WILLIAMS	You pay him then. That's a perilous shot out of an elder-gun, that a poor and private displeasure can do against a monarch! you may as well go about to turn the sun to ice with fanning in his face with a peacock's feather. You'll never trust his word after! come, 'tis a foolish saying.
KING HENRY V	Your reproof is something too round: I should be angry with you, if the time were convenient.
WILLIAMS	Let it be a quarrel between us, if you live.
KING HENRY V	I embrace it.
WILLIAMS	How shall I know thee again?
KING HENRY V	Give me any gage of thine, and I will wear it in my bonnet: then, if ever thou darest acknowledge it, I will make it my quarrel.
WILLIAMS	Here's my glove: give me another of thine.
KING HENRY V	There.
WILLIAMS	This will I also wear in my cap: if ever thou come to me and say, after to-morrow, 'This is my glove,' by this hand, I will take thee a box on the ear.
KING HENRY V	If ever I live to see it, I will challenge it.
WILLIAMS	Thou darest as well be hanged.
KING HENRY V	Well. I will do it, though I take thee in the king's company.

WILLIAMS Keep thy word: fare thee well.

BATES Be friends, you English fools, be friends: we have French quarrels enow, if you could tell how to reckon.

KING HENRY V Indeed, the French may lay twenty French crowns to one, they will beat us; for they bear them on their shoulders: but it is no English treason to cut French crowns, and to-morrow the king himself will be a clipper.

[Exeunt soldiers]

Upon the king! let us our lives, our souls,
Our debts, our careful wives,
Our children and our sins lay on the king!
We must bear all. O hard condition,
Twin-born with greatness, subject to the breath
Of every fool, whose sense no more can feel
But his own wringing! What infinite heart's-ease
Must kings neglect, that private men enjoy!
And what have kings, that privates have not too,
Save ceremony, save general ceremony?
And what art thou, thou idle ceremony?
What kind of god art thou, that suffer'st more
Of mortal griefs than do thy worshippers?
What are thy rents? what are thy comings in?
O ceremony, show me but thy worth!
What is thy soul of adoration?
Art thou aught else but place, degree and form,
Creating awe and fear in other men?
Wherein thou art less happy being fear'd
Than they in fearing.
What drink'st thou oft, instead of homage sweet,
But poison'd flattery? O, be sick, great greatness,
And bid thy ceremony give thee cure!
Think'st thou the fiery fever will go out
With titles blown from adulation?
Will it give place to flexure and low bending?
Canst thou, when thou command'st the beggar's knee,
Command the health of it? No, thou proud dream,
That play'st so subtly with a king's repose;
I am a king that find thee, and I know
'Tis not the balm, the sceptre and the ball,
The sword, the mace, the crown imperial,
The intertissued robe of gold and pearl,
The farced title running 'fore the king,
The throne he sits on, nor the tide of pomp
That beats upon the high shore of this world,
No, not all these, thrice-gorgeous ceremony,
Not all these, laid in bed majestical,
Can sleep so soundly as the wretched slave,
Who with a body fill'd and vacant mind

Gets him to rest, cramm'd with distressful bread;
Never sees horrid night, the child of hell,
But, like a lackey, from the rise to set
Sweats in the eye of Phoebus and all night
Sleeps in Elysium; next day after dawn,
Doth rise and help Hyperion to his horse,
And follows so the ever-running year,
With profitable labour, to his grave:
And, but for ceremony, such a wretch,
Winding up days with toil and nights with sleep,
Had the fore-hand and vantage of a king.
The slave, a member of the country's peace,
Enjoys it; but in gross brain little wots
What watch the king keeps to maintain the peace,
Whose hours the peasant best advantages.

[Enter ERPINGHAM]

ERPINGHAM My lord, your nobles, jealous of your absence,
Seek through your camp to find you.

KING HENRY V Good old knight,
Collect them all together at my tent:
I'll be before thee.

ERPINGHAM I shall do't, my lord. [Exit]

KING HENRY V O God of battles! steel my soldiers' hearts;
Possess them not with fear; take from them now
The sense of reckoning, if the opposed numbers
Pluck their hearts from them. Not to-day, O Lord,
O, not to-day, think not upon the fault
My father made in compassing the crown!
I Richard's body have interred anew;
And on it have bestow'd more contrite tears
Than from it issued forced drops of blood:
Five hundred poor I have in yearly pay,
Who twice a-day their wither'd hands hold up
Toward heaven, to pardon blood; and I have built
Two chantries, where the sad and solemn priests
Sing still for Richard's soul. More will I do;
Though all that I can do is nothing worth,
Since that my penitence comes after all,
Imploring pardon.

[Enter GLOUCESTER]

GLOUCESTER My liege!

KING HENRY V My brother Gloucester's voice? Ay;
I know thy errand, I will go with thee:
The day, my friends and all things stay for me.

[Exeunt]

If you have studied **Twelfth Night** do this task.

Time allowed: 75 minutes

Your work will be assessed for your knowledge and understanding of the play and the way you express your ideas.

Check your work carefully.

Twelfth Night
Act 3 Scene 1
Task

- Describe how Shakespeare uses various types of comedy in this scene.
- Which types of comedy do you think are more effective for today's audience? Give your reasons.

Before you begin to write you should think about:

- What is amusing about the storyline and the theme of confusion.
- What is amusing about what the Clown says and why.
- What is amusing about the characters and how they are portrayed.
- What makes aspects of the comedy difficult for us to appreciate today.

Read the task again before you begin to write your answer.

EXAMINER'S TIPS

Remind yourself about some of the following points:

- Set the scene in the context of the rest of the play. This scene shows the audience how the confusion caused by disguise can be amusing; Shakespeare uses irony.
- Viola is disguised as a boy and has fallen in love with the Duke, Orsino, but of course she cannot tell him. Orsino has started to confide in Cesario (Viola) and to talk about his feelings – this is painful to Viola but amusing to the audience who know about the disguise.
- The Dukes sends Cesario to give messages to Olivia, but unfortunately Olivia falls in love with Cesario (a girl in disguise). Viola needs to be careful in what she says to Olivia – 'I pity you.'
- Viola jokes with the Clown, playing with words.
- The situation with Sir Andrew being fooled into believing that Olivia loves him by Sir Toby is amusing.

Twelfth Night

From Act 3 Scene 1

OLIVIA'S GARDEN

[Enter VIOLA, and Clown with a tabour]

VIOLA Save thee, friend, and thy music: dost thou live by thy tabour?

Clown No, sir, I live by the church.

VIOLA Art thou a churchman?

Clown No such matter, sir: I do live by the church; for I do live at my house, and my house doth stand by the church.

VIOLA So thou mayst say, the king lies by a beggar, if a beggar dwell near him; or, the church stands by thy tabour, if thy tabour stand by the church.

Clown You have said, sir. To see this age! A sentence is but a cheveril glove to a good wit: how quickly the wrong side may be turned outward!

VIOLA Nay, that's certain; they that dally nicely with words may quickly make them wanton.

Clown I would, therefore, my sister had had no name, sir.

VIOLA Why, man?

Clown Why, sir, her name's a word; and to dally with that word might make my sister wanton. But indeed words are very rascals since bonds disgraced them.

VIOLA Thy reason, man?

Clown Troth, sir, I can yield you none without words; and words are grown so false, I am loath to prove reason with them.

VIOLA I warrant thou art a merry fellow and carest for nothing.

Clown Not so, sir, I do care for something; but in my conscience, sir, I do not care for you: if that be to care for nothing, sir, I would it would make you invisible.

VIOLA Art not thou the Lady Olivia's fool?

Clown No, indeed, sir; the Lady Olivia has no folly: she will keep no fool, sir, till she be married; and fools are as like husbands as pilchards are to herrings; the husband's the bigger: I am indeed not her fool, but her corrupter of words.

VIOLA I saw thee late at the Count Orsino's.

Clown	Foolery, sir, does walk about the orb like the sun, it shines every where. I would be sorry, sir, but the fool should be as oft with your master as with my mistress: I think I saw your wisdom there.
VIOLA	Nay, an thou pass upon me, I'll no more with thee. Hold, there's expenses for thee.
Clown	Now Jove, in his next commodity of hair, send thee a beard!
VIOLA	By my troth, I'll tell thee, I am almost sick for one; [Aside] though I would not have it grow on my chin. Is thy lady within?
Clown	Would not a pair of these have bred, sir?
VIOLA	Yes, being kept together and put to use.
Clown	I would play Lord Pandarus of Phrygia, sir, to bring a Cressida to this Troilus.
VIOLA	I understand you, sir; 'tis well begged.
Clown	The matter, I hope, is not great, sir, begging but a beggar: Cressida was a beggar. My lady is within, sir. I will construe to them whence you come; who you are and what you would are out of my welkin, I might say 'element,' but the word is over-worn.
	[Exit]
VIOLA	This fellow is wise enough to play the fool; And to do that well craves a kind of wit: He must observe their mood on whom he jests, The quality of persons, and the time, And, like the haggard, check at every feather That comes before his eye. This is a practice As full of labour as a wise man's art For folly that he wisely shows is fit; But wise men, folly-fall'n, quite taint their wit.
	[Enter SIR TOBY BELCH, and SIR ANDREW]
SIR TOBY BELCH	Save you, gentleman.
VIOLA	And you, sir.
SIR ANDREW	Dieu vous garde, monsieur.
VIOLA	Et vous aussi; votre serviteur.
SIR ANDREW	I hope, sir, you are; and I am yours.
SIR TOBY BELCH	Will you encounter the house? my niece is desirous you should enter, if your trade be to her.

VIOLA I am bound to your niece, sir; I mean, she is the list of my voyage.

SIR TOBY BELCH Taste your legs, sir; put them to motion.

VIOLA My legs do better understand me, sir, than I understand what you mean by bidding me taste my legs.

SIR TOBY BELCH I mean, to go, sir, to enter.

VIOLA I will answer you with gait and entrance. But we are prevented.

[Enter OLIVIA and MARIA]

Most excellent accomplished lady, the heavens rain odours on you!

SIR ANDREW That youth's a rare courtier: 'Rain odours;' well.

VIOLA My matter hath no voice, to your own most pregnant and vouchsafed ear.

SIR ANDREW 'Odours,' 'pregnant' and 'vouchsafed:' I'll get 'em all three all ready.

OLIVIA Let the garden door be shut, and leave me to my hearing.

[Exeunt SIR TOBY BELCH, SIR ANDREW, and MARIA]

Give me your hand, sir.

VIOLA My duty, madam, and most humble service.

OLIVIA What is your name?

VIOLA Cesario is your servant's name, fair princess.

OLIVIA My servant, sir! 'Twas never merry world
Since lowly feigning was call'd compliment:
You're servant to the Count Orsino, youth.

VIOLA And he is yours, and his must needs be yours:
Your servant's servant is your servant, madam.

OLIVIA For him, I think not on him: for his thoughts,
Would they were blanks, rather than fill'd with me!

VIOLA Madam, I come to whet your gentle thoughts
On his behalf.

OLIVIA O, by your leave, I pray you,
I bade you never speak again of him:
But, would you undertake another suit,
I had rather hear you to solicit that
Than music from the spheres.

VIOLA Dear lady, –

OLIVIA Give me leave, beseech you. I did send,
After the last enchantment you did here,
A ring in chase of you: so did I abuse
Myself, my servant and, I fear me, you:
Under your hard construction must I sit,
To force that on you, in a shameful cunning,
Which you knew none of yours: what might you think?
Have you not set mine honour at the stake
And baited it with all the unmuzzled thoughts
That tyrannous heart can think? To one of your receiving
Enough is shown: a cypress, not a bosom,
Hideth my heart. So, let me hear you speak.

VIOLA I pity you.

OLIVIA That's a degree to love.

VIOLA No, not a grize; for 'tis a vulgar proof,
That very oft we pity enemies.

OLIVIA Why, then, methinks 'tis time to smile again.
O, world, how apt the poor are to be proud!
If one should be a prey, how much the better
To fall before the lion than the wolf!

[Clock strikes]

The clock upbraids me with the waste of time.
Be not afraid, good youth, I will not have you:
And yet, when wit and youth is come to harvest,
Your wife is alike to reap a proper man:
There lies your way, due west.

VIOLA Then westward-ho! Grace and good disposition
Attend your ladyship!
You'll nothing, madam, to my lord by me?

OLIVIA Stay:
I prithee, tell me what thou thinkest of me.

VIOLA That you do think you are not what you are.

OLIVIA If I think so, I think the same of you.

VIOLA Then think you right: I am not what I am.

OLIVIA I would you were as I would have you be!

VIOLA Would it be better, madam, than I am?
I wish it might, for now I am your fool.

OLIVIA O, what a deal of scorn looks beautiful
In the contempt and anger of his lip!

Macbeth

English Test Paper 2

If you have studied **Macbeth** do this task.

Time allowed: 75 minutes

Your work will be assessed for your knowledge and understanding of the play and the way you express your ideas.

Check your work carefully.

Macbeth
From Act 3 Scene 4
Task
The play is about evil and the consequences of evil actions.

- Show how this scene is a result of Macbeth's evil acts and that nothing will be the same again for Macbeth and his wife.

Before you begin to write you should think about:

- What Macbeth has had to do to become king.
- What effect this has had on the relationship between him and his wife.
- Why Banquo and his son are a threat to Macbeth and what he does about this.
- The appearance of the ghost in the scene and how Macbeth reacts.
- Who takes control of the situation.
- What Macbeth decides to do as a result of this scene and what happens because of his actions.

Read the task again before you begin to write your answer.

EXAMINER'S TIPS

Remind yourself about some of the following points:

- Set the scene in the context of the rest of the play. Macbeth has murdered Duncan and is now king. For the most part he has stopped taking his wife's advice. He seems in control.
- He has just ordered murderers to kill Banquo, who is a threat to him because Banquo's sons will be kings. Banquo is meant to come to the banquet, but only Macbeth knows he will not. He hopes that Fleance will also be killed, but he escapes.
- Every time Banquo's name is mentioned the ghost appears, tormenting Macbeth, who loses control. No one else can see the ghost, which seems to be a reflection of Macbeth's guilty conscience like the 'dagger' earlier in the play.
- Lady Macbeth takes control of the situation once again, but Macbeth realises that 'blood will have blood' – that he has gone so far that he cannot return: 'I am in blood/Stepped so far …'
- He must revenge himself on Macduff; he does this by killing Macduff's wife and children; and he must return to the witches to ask for their help.
- Lady Macbeth will not be involved from now on. The next time we see her she is mad. Macbeth comes to the conclusion 'we are but young in deed.'

Macbeth

From Act 3, Scene 4

[The GHOST OF BANQUO enters, and sits in MACBETH's place]

MACBETH	Here had we now our country's honour roof'd, Were the graced person of our Banquo present; Who may I rather challenge for unkindness Than pity for mischance!
ROSS	His absence, sir, Lays blame upon his promise. Please't your highness To grace us with your royal company?
MACBETH	The table's full.
LENNOX	Here is a place reserved, sir.
MACBETH	Where?
LENNOX	Here, my good lord. What is't that moves your highness?
MACBETH	Which of you have done this?
Lords	What, my good lord?
MACBETH	Thou canst not say I did it: never shake Thy gory locks at me.
ROSS	Gentlemen, rise: his highness is not well.
LADY MACBETH	Sit, worthy friends: my lord is often thus, And hath been from his youth: pray you, keep seat; The fit is momentary; upon a thought He will again be well: if much you note him, You shall offend him and extend his passion: Feed, and regard him not. Are you a man?
MACBETH	Ay, and a bold one, that dare look on that Which might appal the devil.
LADY MACBETH	O proper stuff! This is the very painting of your fear: This is the air-drawn dagger which, you said, Led you to Duncan. O, these flaws and starts, Impostors to true fear, would well become A woman's story at a winter's fire, Authorized by her grandam. Shame itself! Why do you make such faces? When all's done, You look but on a stool.
MACBETH	Prithee, see there! behold! look! lo! how say you? Why, what care I? If thou canst nod, speak too. If charnel-houses and our graves must send Those that we bury back, our monuments Shall be the maws of kites.

[GHOST OF BANQUO vanishes]

LADY MACBETH What, quite unmann'd in folly?

MACBETH If I stand here, I saw him.

LADY MACBETH Fie, for shame!

MACBETH Blood hath been shed ere now, i' the olden time,
Ere human statute purged the gentle weal;
Ay, and since too, murders have been perform'd
Too terrible for the ear: the times have been,
That, when the brains were out, the man would die,
And there an end; but now they rise again,
With twenty mortal murders on their crowns,
And push us from our stools: this is more strange
Than such a murder is.

LADY MACBETH My worthy lord,
Your noble friends do lack you.

MACBETH I do forget.
Do not muse at me, my most worthy friends,
I have a strange infirmity, which is nothing
To those that know me. Come, love and health to all;
Then I'll sit down. Give me some wine; fill full.
I drink to the general joy o' the whole table,
And to our dear friend Banquo, whom we miss;
Would he were here! to all, and him, we thirst,
And all to all.

Lords Our duties, and the pledge.

[Re-enter GHOST OF BANQUO]

MACBETH Avaunt! and quit my sight! let the earth hide thee!
Thy bones are marrowless, thy blood is cold;
Thou hast no speculation in those eyes
Which thou dost glare with!

LADY MACBETH Think of this, good peers,
But as a thing of custom: 'tis no other;
Only it spoils the pleasure of the time.

MACBETH What man dare, I dare:
Approach thou like the rugged Russian bear,
The arm'd rhinoceros, or the Hyrcan tiger;
Take any shape but that, and my firm nerves
Shall never tremble: or be alive again,
And dare me to the desert with thy sword;
If trembling I inhabit then, protest me
The baby of a girl. Hence, horrible shadow!
Unreal mockery, hence!

[GHOST OF BANQUO vanishes]

Why, so: being gone,
I am a man again. Pray you, sit still.

LADY MACBETH You have displaced the mirth, broke the good meeting,
With most admired disorder.

MACBETH Can such things be,
And overcome us like a summer's cloud,
Without our special wonder? You make me strange
Even to the disposition that I owe,
When now I think you can behold such sights,
And keep the natural ruby of your cheeks,
When mine is blanched with fear.

ROSS What sights, my lord?

LADY MACBETH I pray you, speak not; he grows worse and worse;
Question enrages him. At once, good night:
Stand not upon the order of your going,
But go at once.

LENNOX Good night; and better health
Attend his majesty!

LADY MACBETH A kind good night to all!

[Exeunt all but MACBETH and LADY MACBETH]

MACBETH It will have blood; they say, blood will have blood:
Stones have been known to move and trees to speak;
Augurs and understood relations have
By magot-pies and choughs and rooks brought forth
The secret'st man of blood. What is the night?

LADY MACBETH Almost at odds with morning, which is which.

MACBETH How say'st thou, that Macduff denies his person
At our great bidding?

LADY MACBETH Did you send to him, sir?

MACBETH I hear it by the way; but I will send:
There's not a one of them but in his house
I keep a servant fee'd. I will to-morrow,
And betimes I will, to the weird sisters:
More shall they speak; for now I am bent to know,
By the worst means, the worst. For mine own good,
All causes shall give way: I am in blood
Stepp'd in so far that, should I wade no more,
Returning were as tedious as go o'er:
Strange things I have in head, that will to hand;
Which must be acted ere they may be scann'd.

LADY MACBETH You lack the season of all natures, sleep.

MACBETH Come, we'll to sleep. My strange and self-abuse
Is the initiate fear that wants hard use:
We are yet but young in deed.

[Exeunt]

English Test Answers

Paper 1

It is difficult to mark answers in an English test because the questions are often open to interpretation. Examiners for the English paper do not have a rigid mark scheme, but they will have a core of important points which will need to be covered to achieve a particular score. There is not an expectation that a candidate will find 'all the points'. Marking is focused on the 'impression' created by the answer.

A mark scheme is provided for each question. You will need to judge how well the points made in the answer match with the score criteria. Any point should be clearly stated. The most effective way of assessing work at home is to mark the piece together so both can see how the final score can be calculated. This will involve discussion of what is in the answer and what has been omitted and so can form a learning experience in itself.

Question 1

a) Give 5 marks for identifying all eight items.

1. Paper hangings (streamers) for round the legs
2. An apron made from paper
3. Tinsel bows
4. A tinsel heart
5. Green and red tinsel rosettes
6. Bows for the arms
7. A black mask with horns
8. A small guy made from patchwork quilting filled with sawdust

b) Give 5 marks for fulfilling all these criteria.

- The list above should be used as the basis for the instructions.
- Instructions should be written in chronological order and use command verbs and suitable connectives, e.g. 'First take some paper streamers and wrap them around the legs. Then…'.
- Quotation should be used where necessary, e.g. Place a black mask on the boy's face 'with a little red on the cheek' so he looks like the devil to scare people.

Score	National Curriculum Level
9–10	Level 7+
7–8	Level 7
5–6	Level 6
3–4	Level 5
1–2	Level 4 or below

Question 2

Give one mark for each of the following points made.

- He does not always speak in complete sentences: 'Said it was a disgrace'.
- We get a sense of him through his use of slang: 'chucked money … they chiselled me'.
- He is direct in what he says – tells you his age straight away and how he feels about things.
- We feel somewhat sorry for the character as his father has died, but it seems very matter of fact to him – a feature of street life in nineteenth-century London.
- He seems like a 'typical' teenager, e.g. his father disagreed with how he spent his time: 'He didn't like it at all'.
- He seems to enjoy the festival – there is a sense of excitement in how he describes how they dress him: 'it looked stunnin''.
- He is used to street life: 'one of our chaps knew what they were after'.
- He is sensible enough to 'keep still' when the muggers appear but runs with the rest of them, and common sense is shown in the way he refuses to do this again and is aware that he has been cheated.

Score	National Curriculum Level
8	Level 7+
6–7	Level 7
5	Level 6
3–4	Level 5
1–2	Level 4 or below

Question 3

c) Award one mark for each of the following points made.

- The poet describes the fireworks as magic flowers – 'orchids' – which are beautiful, exotic and showy.
- They 'flower' because they are described as 'buds' earlier – they look like something dull, curled up or rolled up, but they soon change into something more exciting.
- He continues the imagery with 'fiery petals' – parts of the firework explode and drop to the earth as petals would fall from a flower. The sparks of the fireworks become 'golden grain'.
- They slowly change into weapons – 'rockets… shocked with blast… cannon' – and the fire seems sinister: 'greedy flames… spit of fire…'
- The garden starts as 'dark' and then becomes a 'frenzied' place for a while, full of bright light and noise – 'squealing high'. People run about in excitement 'helter-skelter' and the children speak excitedly.
- As well as seeing the fireworks, we can feel the heat, hear the noise and smell the smoke.

d) Award one mark for each of the following points made.

- The starting point of the bad memory is 'cannon' – a kind of firework but also a gun used in war.
- The imagery changes from that of beauty into something more like that expected in war – 'bangs… bitter scent… banshee howl of mortar… torn earth's grunts'.

- All his senses remind him of a time when he fought in the war – ten years ago, 'a ten-year memory'. He has a sudden flashback which spoils the party atmosphere. He is afraid: 'taste my fear'.
- The children with him are the children of someone who died in the war – 'a corpse's sons'. The irony is that as innocent children they do not understand why their uncle should be afraid.

Score	National Curriculum Level
9–10	Level 7+
7–8	Level 7
5–6	Level 6
3–4	Level 5
1–2	Level 4 or below

Question 4 (Writing Test)

This question is marked for overall impression – there is not a set of correct points which should be incorporated. Both content and how the content is communicated – style, grammar, punctuation, accuracy – are considered.

However there is a set of marking criteria which needs to be considered. Assess the work for each criterion and award an appropriate mark.

Does the answer:	Yes	No	Possible mark
Communicate ideas clearly to you?			6
Use a suitable style for the purpose indicated in the question?			6
Organise the material in an appropriate way to the style?			6
Use paragraphs, correct grammar and punctuation?			6
Spell words correctly and make use of relevant words precisely?			6
Look neat and make reading easy?			2

Score	National Curriculum Level
30–32	Level 7+
24–29	Level 7
18–23	Level 6
13–17	Level 5
7–12	Level 4 or below

Answers

All Shakespeare plays – Paper 2

This paper is marked for:

- **Understanding and Response.** What is written. This tests understanding of **the Shakespeare play**, its characters, its themes and story as well as its language.
- **Written Expression.** How it is written. This tests the candidate's ability to write clear answers about **the Shakespeare play** in clear, logical, grammatically correct English.

According to the official mark scheme there are 40 marks available for the Shakespeare section of the test.

- **Understanding and Response will be marked out of 24**

21–24 marks	Exceptional performance	Above Level 7
17–20 marks	Well above average	Level 7
13–16 marks	Above average	Level 6
9–12 marks	Average/below average	Level 5
4–8 marks	Well below average	Level 4 and below

- **Written Expression will be marked out of 16. See page 75 for details of this.**

Answers should include these key points, illustrated by suitable quotations.

Henry V

Key points – look for at least 6 of these and mark each out of 4

- In this scene, we see Henry as a vulnerable human being, not a protected king. He walks – 'a little touch of Harry in the night' – among his troops on the eve of the battle of Agincourt where the English are likely to be defeated. At Agincourt it seems the British are heavily outnumbered 'five to one' and very tired. How can they possibly win the battle? Because of the riotous times of his youth Henry has had to prove to his men and to his country that he is a fit king.
- His men are critical of the king: he 'has a heavy reckoning to make'. He will be responsible for any the deaths in the battle. Henry has to understand this but allows that although 'every subject's duty is the king's; but every subject's soul is his own'. Every man must believe in what he is fighting for.
- Williams argues with 'Le Roy' about the king's responsibility and they promise to fight later, with Williams wearing one of the king's gloves as a remembrance. Later the king has some sport with this but rewards Williams for his honesty and bravery – again the response of a person with humanity, who understand his people, and not a 'distant' and aloof King.
- Henry's soliloquy reflects upon 'the hard position' of being a king. Kings 'neglect what private men enjoy'. We know he has lived the life of many of these men in his youth so we can see that he has been equipped to rule his subjects fairly. There is no rest for the king. He cannot 'sleep so sound as the wretched slave'.
- Henry prays to the 'God of battles' for assistance. He is a clever tactician and knows that the only way to win this battle is to have a solid group of men who really want to fight – and possibly die for him: 'Five hundred poor I have in yearly pay.' He wants no half-hearted troops.
- He appeals directly to their sense of patriotism. Those who fight alongside him on this day will become legends in their own right. He will not give up his 'honour'. He would rather fight: 'I would not lose so great an honour'; he would not want to share this with anyone else. He immediately makes his men seem on the same level as he – they are all soldiers together.
- He gives his men the opportunity to leave – although to do so would appear cowardly: 'he which hath no stomach for the fight/Let him depart'. He even offers them money for their journey home. He ensures that all those who will fight are completely committed to the battle.
- His emotional appeal is to their 'fellowship to die with us'. He recalls the day 'the feast of Crispian' and makes a case that all who fight today will become the stuff of legend in England, whether they die or not. They will become 'we happy few, we band of brothers'.
- Henry is calm but confident. He shows his men that love of their king and their country will be great in terms of 'honour'. The fighters will be remembered and even envied; men who were not there will 'hold their manhoods cheap whiles any speaks/That fought with us upon Saint Crispin's day'. In this way he is personally responsible for the victory.

Twelfth Night

Key points – look for at least 6 of these and mark each out of 4

- This scene shows Viola returning to Olivia's house to continue with the Duke's wooing. While she waits for Olivia, the Clown and Viola joke together.
- The Duke Orsino thinks that Cesario, his trusted page, is a boy; he is not aware that 'he' is Viola in disguise. He has sent Viola, as a boy, to 'woo' Olivia for him, as Olivia has previously stated that she would have nothing to do with him. Olivia, however, falls in love with Cesario (as a boy). To add to the confusion, Viola (Cesario) has fallen in love with the Duke, but naturally (because of her disguise) cannot reveal her feelings.
- The Clown is often seen as 'a fool' but he is one of the only people in the play who sees beyond disguise and the confusion, 'What's a drunken man like, fool? …', 'Like a drowned man …', 'Lady Olivia will keep no fool.' The first kind of comedy is the comedy of language. They joke and play with the meaning of words, 'dost thou live by thy tabour? No sir, I live by the church.' The Clown spends his time trying to get Viola to give him money and jokes arise from this: 'Would not a pair of these have bred, sir?'
- Another form of humour is irony. The characters in disguise comment on one another's words (which have a different meaning to the audience). The Clown jokes with Viola, who he thinks is a young boy: 'Now Jove … send thee a beard.' We know Viola's comments have more to do with her being a young woman: 'I am almost sick for one.'
- Characters are also amusing. Sir Andrew is a fool and his comments on the use of courtly language by Viola are amusing: 'That youth's a rare courtier', 'Rain odours' well.' Sir Toby is a strong, blustering character and his lines are more aggressive.
- When Olivia enters, the situation itself becomes comic. We know she is in love with another woman (thinking she is a man), so whatever she says becomes amusing. Olivia has sent Viola a ring to ensure that she returns, and Viola tries to ensure that she is not attractive to Olivia – 'I pity you' – but nothing seems to work – 'O what a deal of scorn looks beautiful ..'
- Olivia thinks Viola (Cesario) is in love with her. The theme of confusion and disguise creates humour on the stage. We, as the audience are aware of the situation – the characters are not. This is also irony.
- The most difficult form of comedy for us today is the comedy of language, because many of the words used by Shakespeare are not known to us today. This comedy was an intellectual comedy, very popular in the seventeenth century but less popular with us. Visual comedy – disguise and confusion – is still popular, since we understand the situations. The characters are well drawn in Shakespeare, and we understand their motivation and their foibles, because the same characters could exist today.

Macbeth

Key points – look for at least 6 of these and mark each out of 4

- In this scene, Macbeth is now king. He has murdered Duncan and the Duncan's sons have fled. However, he does not yet feel secure because of the witches' prophecy for Banquo, 'Thou shalt get kings, though thou shall be none.' Macbeth has hired murderers to kill Banquo and his son Fleance.
- Macbeth's alibi is that he is present at the banquet. Banquo is dead 'with twenty trenched gashes on his head', but Fleance has escaped: 'now am I cabined, cribbed, confined …' All the lords and Lady Macbeth await Banquo's return from hunting. Only Macbeth knows that he will not be there and have to play the hypocrite.
- The ghost appears twice during the banquet and only Macbeth can see it. It appears every time Banquo's name is mentioned: 'were the graced person of Banquo present …'. It is almost as if Macbeth's hypocrisy causes the apparition to appear. The ghost sits in his chair, and Macbeth's reaction must seem very strange to the other lords: 'never shake/Thy gory locks at me.'
- Lady Macbeth has seen this side of Macbeth's character before. At key moments of crisis, his conscience tends to conjure up images: 'this is the air-drawn dagger which, you said/Led you to Duncan … You look but upon a stool.' His wife takes control of the situation once again, as she had to do when Macbeth brought the daggers away from the scene of the crime, having murdered Duncan. This is the last time in the play when she will take control. The next time we see her she is mad, talking in her sleep, her awareness of her part in the evil deeds too much for her.
- Macbeth calms himself but makes the mistake of pretending that he wished 'our good friend Banquo' in the room. The ghost appears again, and once more Macbeth is seen raving at thin air. 'Avaunt! And quit my sight.' His wife once again calms the assembled lords by making excuses: 'Think of this good peers …' The ghost disappears and Macbeth asserts 'I am a man again'.
- But it is too late: 'You have displaced the mirth' says his wife, and the lords are dismissed. When they are alone Macbeth knows that 'blood will have blood'. He has murdered once and he now realises he cannot stop murdering if he is to remain secure on the throne. Macduff 'denies his person/At our great bidding.' He has fled to England and is now a threat. Later Macbeth will kill Macduff's wife and children.
- We see how Macbeth has changed in his insecurity. He has spies everywhere, 'There's not one of them but in his house/I keep a servant fee'd.' He also realises that he must again seek the help of the witches. This indicates the extent to which evil has taken him over. Previously the witches looked for him; now he will seek them out.
- Most importantly, things will never be the same again because,

'I am in blood
Stepp'd in so far, should I wade no more,
Returning were as tedious as go o'er'
He has nothing left to lose. He is isolated now and 'yet but young in deed.'

Checklist for assessing written expression

Work through the list until you answer 'No'. This is the level of attainment.

Level 4	**Yes**	**No**	**Mark**
Ideas clearly expressed			4
Paragraphs – organised ideas			
Punctuation to separate sentences generally accurate			
Spelling of simple words accurate			
Handwriting clear and legible			

Level 5	**Yes**	**No**	
Ideas clearly expressed			8
Wide vocabulary and precise use of words			
Simple and complex sentences used – made into paragraphs			
Variety of punctuation – apostrophes and commas used correctly			
Spelling words – complex regular patterns accurate			
Handwriting – clear, legible, fluent			

Level 6	**Yes**	**No**	
Ideas clearly expressed with a sense of purpose			12
A varied vocabulary used – appropriate language expressed in simple and complex sentences with good paragraphing			
Spelling accurate – some difficult words still incorrect			
Range of punctuation used – some more difficult forms			
Handwriting fluent and legible			

Level 7	**Yes**	**No**	
Confidently expressed ideas – words chosen are appropriate			16
Appropriate style is matched by appropriate language			
Accurate grammar and punctuation are consciously used for effect			
Correct paragraphing			
Correct spelling of irregular words			
Handwriting consistently fluent and legible			

Those achieving levels below level 4 or above level 7 should be obvious from their work if assessed on this chart. Those achieving above level 7 could be taking a supplementary test paper. Those achieving level 3 should be taking a special paper. It is best to consult the student's teacher.

National Curriculum Levels

The chart below will give an indication of performance in the combined English tests and provide a National Curriculum level.

Because the exam criteria for marking will change from year to year, dependent on the difficulty of the test and the candidates involved, it is impossible to make this process exact.

Total the marks which have been given for both papers. The score will be out of 100.

- Paper 1 is marked out of 60.
- Paper 2 is marked out of 40.

Combined score of Papers 1 and 2	**Approximate National Curriculum Level**
29 and below	Below Level 4
30 – 45	Level 4
46 – 60	Level 5
61 – 75	Level 6
76 – 85	Level 7
86 and above	Above Level 7

Science at Key Stage 3

Preparing for the tests

You can specifically improve your marks by taking into account the following points:

The language used in the questions

1. The examiners will not put any useless information in a question. If something is written down then the examiner wants you to use it.
   Example *Space probes have shown that there are* ***mountains, dry river valleys*** *and* ***volcanoes*** *on Mars. Scientists believe Mars, like Earth, has all three types of rock:* ***igneous, metamorphic*** *and* ***sedimentary***. You will need to use all the terms.
2. Use the mark scheme to tell you how many points you should include in your answers.
3. Read the question very carefully.
   Example *Tick the correct box.* Only tick one box. The mark scheme will probably indicate to the marker that if more than one box has been ticked the question should be marked incorrect.
4. Don't be put off if you encounter unfamiliar material. You will know enough science to answer the question. In the example above you may not know much about Mars. However, the work you have done on rock formation on Earth will let you answer the question.

Key words found in the questions

1. **Choose** from a list of words. Make sure you use words from the list. Unless the paper states otherwise, you can use words more than once. Similarly you don't have to use them all.
2. **Describe...** You do **not** have to explain anything; you simply have to make a physical description of a diagram, graph etc.
   Example If you are asked to describe a graph you might say "From 1950 to 1967 the number of people suffering from measles varied from year to year but overall remained constant at around 5 per 100000. From 1967 to 1981 the number of people suffering from measles again varied from year to year but decreased from around 5 per 100 000 to 1 per 100000." You do not have to explain **why** it remained constant and then decreased.
3. **Explain...** You need to include a scientific explanation for your answer. Include some key scientific words in your answer.
   Example The plant in flask C receives *light*, which it needs for *photosynthesis*.
4. **Predict...** There are two possible types of prediction:
   - Predicting what you think might happen in an investigation.
   - Extrapolating a graph (continuing a trend) to predict what might happen in the future.
5. Be aware of **negatives**.
   Example *Give the name of another metal,* ***not*** *in the table...*
6. **Advantages and disadvantages**. To be on the safe side, make sure you state both things in your comparisons.
   Example *Give* ***one*** *advantage of using biomass rather than fossil fuel as an energy resource.* Energy from biomass is renewable whereas energy from fossil fuels is non-renewable.
7. **Name... Which... What... Give...** These are simple command words which require a simple response. These are often found with numbers or words in bold type.

Sitting the practice tests

Remember that the practice tests are designed to help you to get used to what are sometimes called 'examination conditions'. In other words, when you take the tests in May you will be given an exact time (60 minutes) and be expected to work in silence with no books or other people to help you. That is exactly how you should practise.

1. You need a pencil or pen and a watch or clock.
2. Make sure that you have somewhere quiet to work.
3. Ask someone to time the test so that you have exactly 60 minutes.
4. If you cannot read a scientific word then someone can read it to you. That person should not tell you what it means.
5. Do not rush at the test as soon as the timer starts. Take a few deep breaths and try to relax.
6. Do not start answering the questions until you have had a look at all of the test paper. This will give you a good idea of what is covered in the test and how many questions there are.
7. Read each question carefully and follow the instructions.
8. Do not spend too long over any one question. Answer it and move on.
9. If you can't answer a question, don't worry. Move on to the next one. You can always come back at the end.
10. Try to use all of the time available. If you think you have finished, go back and check every question. Make sure you have not made silly mistakes or missed a question out.
11. At the end of the time, check your answers with the mark scheme and work out your total.
12. Make a list of the questions you did not do too well on, but congratulate yourself on those you answered well.
13. Discuss the questions you found most difficult with a parent or a teacher. It is a good idea to check your notes to make sure that the topic won't cause problems again.

After a few weeks, try the questions again. You will improve your score if you have been working and revising and you will be well prepared for the real thing.

1 The drawing below shows an eagle.

a **i** Name one part of the eagle which it uses to fly.

Wings

ii The eagle has to catch small animals to eat.

Look at the eagle.
Describe two ways in which the eagle is adapted to eat small animals.

1. Pointed beak
2. sharp claws

1

2

TOTAL

3

b The chart shows the food eaten by an eagle.

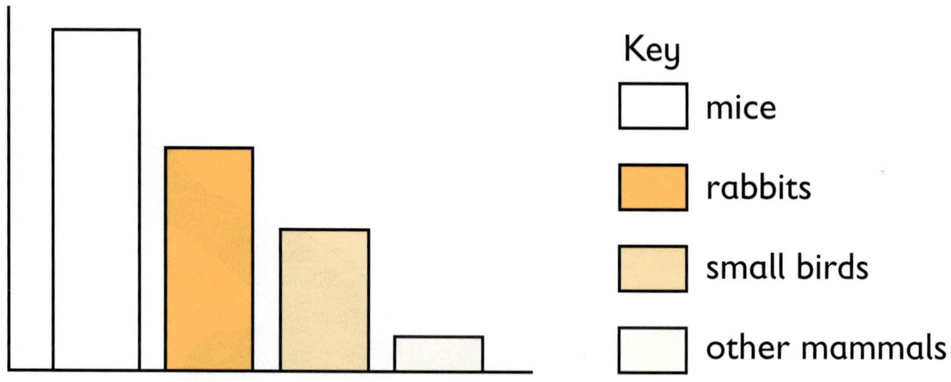

What is the main food eaten by an eagle?

mice

1

c A food chain which ends with the eagle is:

small plant → insect → small bird → eagle

i Which is the primary consumer in this food chain?

insect

ii Which is the producer in this food chain?

small plant

2

TOTAL

3

2 The chart shows one way to group animals with backbones.

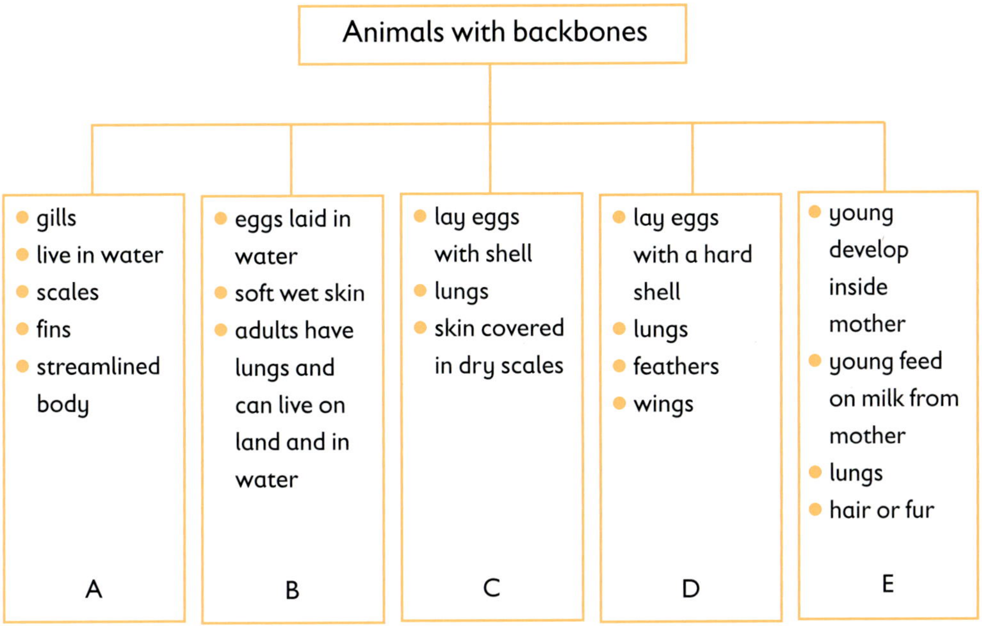

a To which group (A, B, C, D or E) do the following living things belong?
Each letter may be used **once, more than once** or **not at all**.

frog B

goldfish A

snake C

gorilla E

sparrow D

5

b What is the name given to animals with a backbone?
Tick the correct box.

invertebrates ☐

predators ☐

amphibians ☐

vertebrates ☑

1

TOTAL

6

3 The information below was taken from the labels of a packet of breakfast cereal and a tin of cream of tomato soup.

Nutritional Information		
	Cereal per 100 g	**Cream of tomato soup per 100 g**
energy	1440 kj	268 kj
protein	11.2 g	0.9 g
total carbohydrate	67.6 g	7.1 g
sugar	4.7 g	5.3 g
fat	2.7 g	5.3 g
fibre	10.5 g	0.4 g
sodium	0.3 g	0.4 g

a Give **one** reason why we need protein in our diet.

_______________ 1

b Which of the two food substances above provides the most fibre?

Cereal 1

c Give **one** reason why we need fibre in our diet.

_______________ 1

d Which food substance above would provide the most energy for exercise?

Cereal 1

TOTAL 4

4 The following warning sign was on a bottle of acid:

a Tick the correct word from the list below to describe what the symbol means.

1

flammable	☐	poison	☐
corrosive	☐	irritant	✓

b A teacher pours some of the acid onto some magnesium metal to show what will happen. It reacts to give off a gas.

i What would you see in the mixture as the gas is being formed?

1

____

____

ii Write down **two** safety rules which must be followed when using acids.

1

wear goggles

____

TOTAL

3

5 David adds some sugar to his tea.

a Which words in the list below describe the sugar, the tea and the sweet tea?

solvent **solute** **filtrate** **sediment** **solution**

3

substance	word
tea	solvent
sugar	sediment
sweet tea	solution

b David wants to make the sugar dissolve more quickly.
What **two** things could he do?

2

1. make it hotter
2. add more tea

c Is unsweetened tea a pure substance?
Tick the correct box.

2

pure substance ☐ mixture ☑

Explain your answer.

they may need to add other substances to get it unsweetened.

TOTAL

7

6 New buildings do not stay looking new for ever. The weather damages the materials. This is called **weathering**. No materials are taken away. When the material is broken down and then removed, the process is known as **erosion**.

a For the examples shown in the table, tick one box in each row to show if the example is **weathering, erosion** or **neither**.

5

example	weathering	erosion	neither
A new building is still in excellent condition			✓
An old gravestone is breaking into pieces		✓	
A river has washed away part of a road	✓		
Rain has started to weaken a metal bridge	✓		
The brickwork on a school wall has started to crumble		✓	

b How does ice cause damage to rocks?

1

The ice expands forcing the rock to crack

TOTAL

6

7a This table gives some of the properties of metals and non-metals.

metal	non-metal
malleable and ductile	brittle or soft
sonorous (rings when hit)	not sonorous
good electrical conductor	insulator (bad conductor)
good heat conductor	insulator (bad conductor)
surface is shiny	surface is dull
usually high density	low density

From the list of properties give a reason why:

i bells are made of metal

____

____

ii electrical wires are made from metal

____

____

iii electrical plugs are covered in plastic – a non-metal

____

____

iv non-metals are not usually made into jewellery

____

____

4

TOTAL

4

b Some kitchen spoons are made from plastic and metal – usually stainless steel.

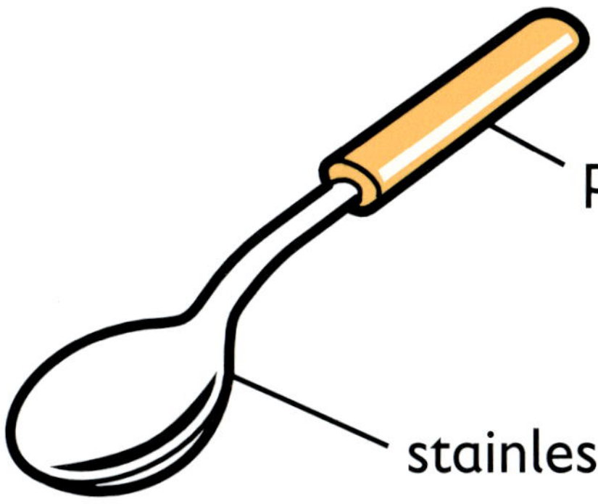

i Give one reason why the handle is made from plastic.

____ 1

ii Give **two** reasons why the spoon is made from stainless steel.

1. ____

2. ____ 2

iii Would you select a metal or a non-metal to make the bottom of a saucepan?

____ 2

Explain your answer.

____

____

TOTAL 5

8 Joanne sets up the circuit shown below.

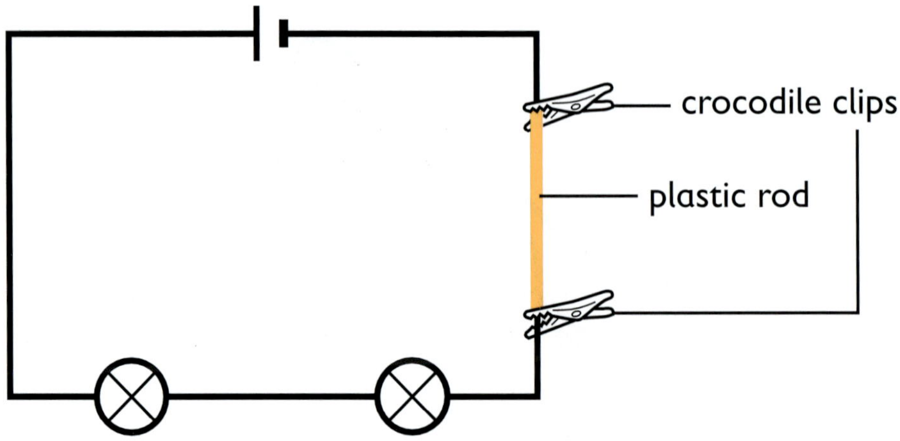

a Why do the two bulbs **not** light up?
Tick the correct box.

The bulbs are connected the wrong way round. ☐

There is a gap in the circuit. ☐

The plastic is a conductor. ☐

The plastic is an insulator. ☐

1

b Joanne replaces the plastic rod with a steel one.

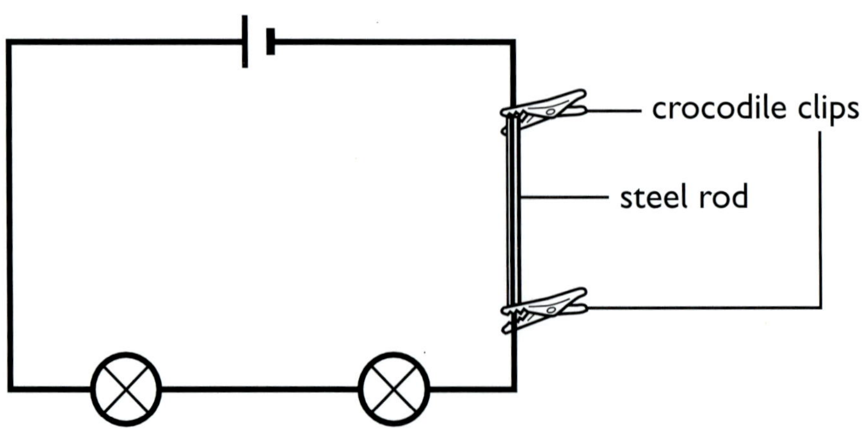

TOTAL

1

Why do the two bulbs light up?

1

c Joanne now tries a range of materials by connecting them between the two crocodile clips. Complete her results table by placing a **tick** in the correct spaces.

5

material	bulbs light	bulbs do not light
aluminium foil		
wood		
paper		
copper		
glass		

TOTAL

6

9 Michael shines his torch onto a white CD cover.

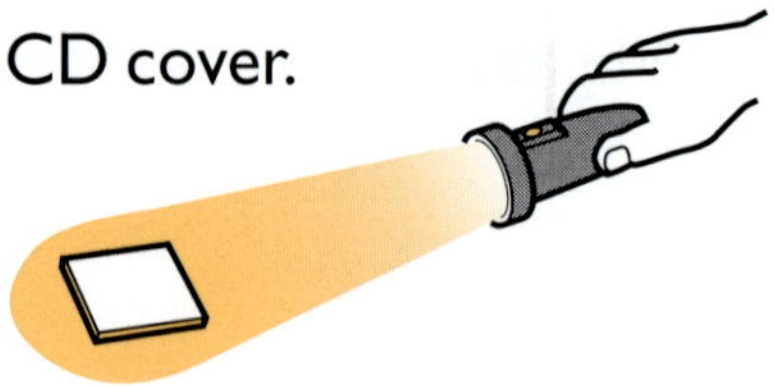

a Describe how light from the torch lights up the CD cover and makes it visible to Michael.

2

b Michael's torch is fitted with coloured filters. He uses it to shine different coloured light onto three of his CD covers.

Complete the table below to show the colours that the covers appear to Michael.

2

colour of CD cover	colour of light	colour the CD cover appears to Michael
white	white	
white	red	
white	green	
green	white	
green	red	
red	white	
red	green	

c What colour would a black CD cover look in any light?

Explain your answer.

2

TOTAL

6

10 The diagram below shows part of a plant root.

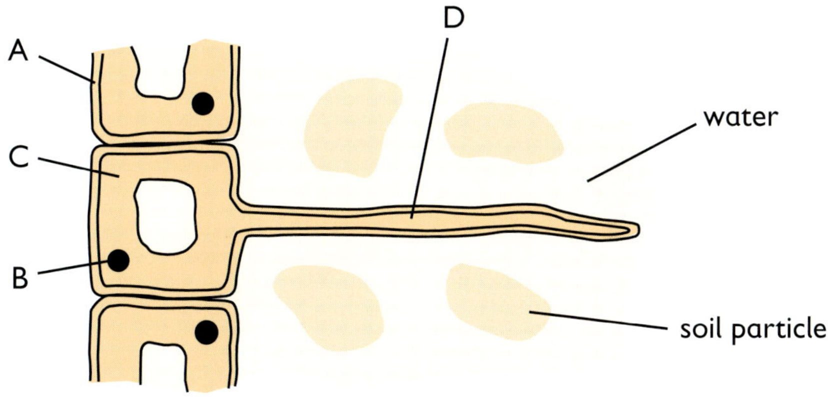

a What are the names of the parts of the plant cells labelled A, B, C and D?

A ______________________________

B ______________________________

C ______________________________

D ______________________________

4

b Write down the importance to the plant cell of the following parts.

Part A is important because ______________________________

____

Part B is important because ______________________________

____

2

c Part D is specially adapted to help the root absorb water. Explain how the adaptation helps the root cell to absorb more water.

____

____

1

TOTAL

7

11 The diagram shows the Earth in orbit around the Sun.

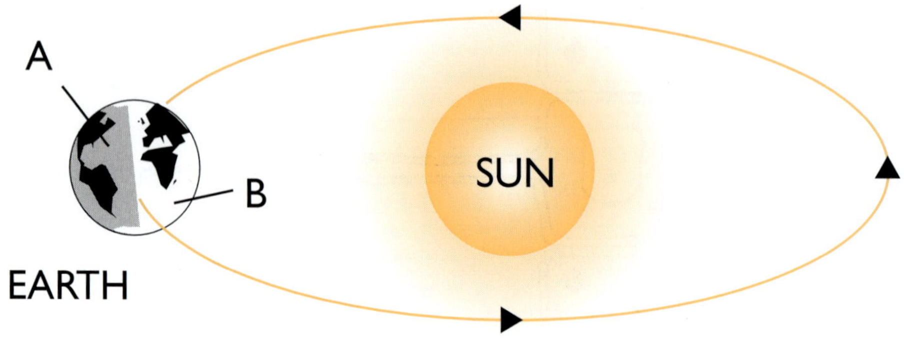

a Give the names of **two** planets in the solar system which are closer to the Sun than the Earth.

1. ______________________

2. ______________________

2

b Give the names of **two** planets in the solar system which are further away from the Sun than the Earth.

1. ______________________

2. ______________________

2

c The distance a planet is from the Sun affects two things: the temperature of the planet and the length of a year (the time it takes the planet to orbit the Sun).

Tick the correct box.

A planet that is near to the Sun will have:

A high surface temperature and a long year ☐

A low surface temperature and a short year ☐

A high surface temperature and a short year ☐

A low surface temperature and a long year ☐

1

TOTAL

5

d Look at the diagram of the Earth and Sun.

i Explain why it is night time at point A.

____

____

1

ii Explain why it is day time at point B.

____

____

1

iii What time will it be at A in 12 hours' time?

____

2

Explain your answer.

____

____

e On the diagram, draw the position of the Earth three months later than shown.

Explain why you have drawn the Earth in this position.

____

____

2

TOTAL

6

12 The diagram shows an experiment with bromine liquid. The liquid is added to a gas jar and observed after 5 minutes.

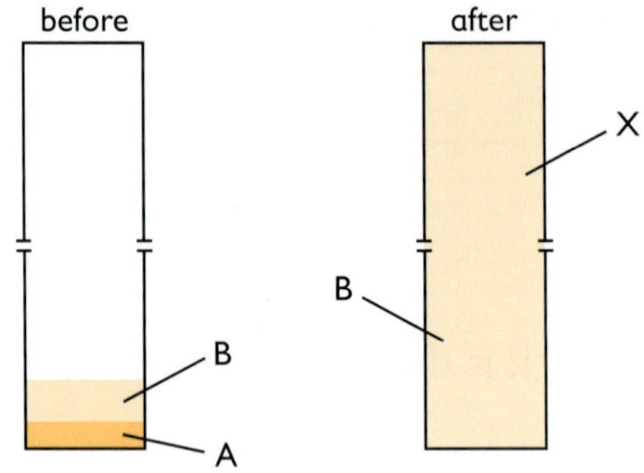

a **i** Which letter on the diagram represents bromine liquid?

____

ii Which letter on the diagram represents bromine vapour?

____

iii Explain why the bromine fills the jar after 5 minutes.

____

____

____

3

b Explain how you can smell food being cooked a long way away.

____

____

1

TOTAL

4

c The box below on the left shows the arrangement of particles in the liquid bromine. In the box on the right, draw the arrangement of particles in the bromine vapour. 1

d Which of the statements below is true about the part of the bromine experiment labelled X? 1
Tick the correct box.

The particles here are all bromine molecules. ☐

The particles here are bromine vapour and bromine liquid. ☐

The particles here are a mixture of air molecules and bromine molecules. ☐

The particles here are all air molecules. ☐

e What is the name of the process whereby a gas or vapour spreads out? 1
Tick the correct box.

freezing	☐	condensation	☐
filtration	☐	diffusion	☐

TOTAL 3

1

13a A piece of coal is an energy resource. How is the energy stored in a piece of coal?

Tick the correct box.

as kinetic energy ☐

as potential energy ☐

as chemical energy ☐

as thermal energy ☐

2

b When coal is burned, energy is transferred from the coal to its surroundings. Complete the boxes below to show the energy change involved.

----------------------------	changes to →	----------------------------
energy in coal		energy

TOTAL

3

c In a coal power station there are many stages between burning the coal and generating the electricity. These stages are shown below.

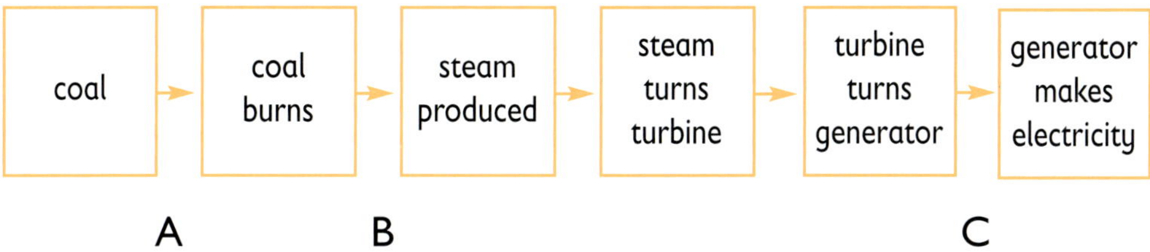

Each of the stages (A, B and C) involves an energy transfer.

i Which letter represents the change

thermal energy ⟶ kinetic energy?

1

ii Which letter represents the change

kinetic energy ⟶ electrical energy?

1

iii Which letter represents the change

chemical energy ⟶ thermal energy?

1

TOTAL

3

Science Test

Answers

Question number	Answer	Mark	Comments and tips
1a	i. Wings ii. Sharp talons to catch prey; sharp, curved beak to tear prey	1 2	
1b	mice	1	
1c	i. insect ii. small plant	2	Producers make food by processing sunlight; consumers are animals that eat producers.
2a	frog – B goldfish – A snake – C gorilla – E sparrow – D	5	
2b	Vertebrates should be ticked.	1	Vertebrate means having a backbone.
3a	To build muscle *or* to make enzymes	1	
3b	Cereal	1	
3c	It helps digestion.	1	
3d	Cereal	1	
4a	Corrosive should be ticked.	1	
4b	Bubbles forming	1	
4c	Any two from: Protect the eyes Replace stoppers Wear gloves Report spills	2	
5a	tea – solvent sugar – solute sweet tea – solution	3	
5b	Any two from: Use smaller lumps of sugar Stir the tea Use hotter water	2	
5c	It is a mixture. It is a mixture of hot water and substances from the tea leaves.	2	

Question number	Answer	Mark	Comments and tips
6a	neither weathering erosion weathering weathering	5	
6b	Water enters cracks and freezes. This ice expands and widens the cracks.	1	
7a	i. Metals are sonorous. ii. Metals conduct electricity. iii. Non-metals are insulators. iv. Non-metals are brittle or soft *or* non-metal surfaces are dull.	4	
7b	i. Plastic is an insulator. ii. Any two from: The steel is malleable (can be shaped) The steel is shiny The steel is hard (has a high density). iii. A metal, because it will conduct heat from the stove.	1 2 2	
8a	The plastic is an insulator.	1	An insulator does not conduct heat or electricity.
8b	Because the steel rod is a conductor of electricity.	1	
8c	aluminium foil – bulbs light wood – bulbs do not light paper – bulbs do not light copper – bulbs light glass – bulbs do not light	5	Aluminium is a conductor.
9a	Light from the torch hits the CD cover and some is reflected back to his eyes.	2	
9b	white red green green black red black	2	
9c	Black The black cover absorbs all the colours of the white light.	2	

Question number	Answer	Mark	Comments and tips
10a	A = cell wall B = nucleus C = cytoplasm D = root hair	4	
10b	Part A (cell wall) helps the cell to maintain its shape. Part B (nucleus) controls the reactions of the cell.	2	
10c	The thin walls and large surface area allow more water to enter.	1	
11a	Mercury and Venus	2	
11b	Any two from: Mars, Jupiter, Saturn, Uranus, Neptune, Pluto	2	
11c	A high surface temperature and a short year	1	
11d	i. A is facing away from the Sun ii. B is facing towards the Sun iii. Day time. The Earth will have turned half way round and so will face the other way.	1 1 2	
11e	The Earth should be drawn directly below the Sun on the diagram. It will have travelled one quarter of its yearly orbit in 3 months.	2	The Earth takes one year to orbit the Sun completely.
12a	i. A ii. B iii. The vapour diffuses to fill the container and mix with the air.	3	
12b	The food gives off small particles which diffuse in the air, reaching your nose.	1	
12c	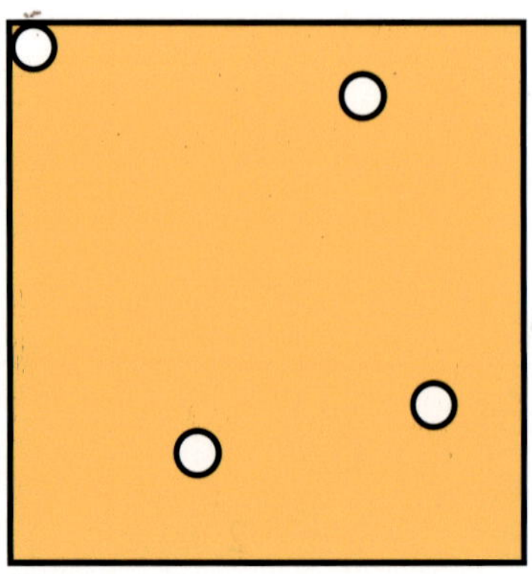	1	The molecules in a liquid are close but free-flowing; those in a gas are far apart.

Question number	Answer	Mark	Comments and tips
12d	The particles here are a mixture of air molecules and bromine molecules.	1	
12e	diffusion	1	
13a	as chemical energy	1	
13b	chemical thermal *or* heat	2	
13c	i. B ii. C iii. A	1 1 1	

National Curriculum Levels

Maximum marks: 86

Mark	0–33	34–46	47–59	60–75	76–86
Level	Below Level 4	Level 4	Level 5	Level 6	Approaching Level 7

If you scored very highly in this test, you could try the Level 4–7 Science paper in the WHSmith Key Stage 3 Maths, English and Science Practice Papers Book 2.

If you need more practice in any Science topics, you should use the WHSmith Key Stage 3 Science Revision Guide.

Notes

Notes